BEETHOVEN

PIANO SONATAS   Op. 14, Nos. 1, 2; Op. 22; Op. 26; Op. 27, Nos. 1, 2; Op. 28

AN ALFRED MASTERWORK EDITION

Cover art: Ludwig van Beethoven *(1770–1827)*
by Karl Stieler (1781–1858)
Oil on canvas, 1819
Beethoven-Haus, Bonn, Germany
Erich Lessing/Art Resource, NY
Additional art: © Planet Art

Supervising Editor: Sharon Aaronson
Music Engraving: Bruce Nelson
Cover Design: Dana D'Elia

Copyright © MMV by Alfred Publishing Co., Inc.
All rights reserved. Printed in USA.
ISBN 0-7390-3762-5

LUDWIG VAN BEETHOVEN

Thematic Index

Sonata No. 9 in E Major, Op. 14, No. 1

.... page 16

Sonata No. 10 in G Major, Op. 14, No. 2

.... page 33

Sonata No. 11 in B-flat Major (Grande Sonate), Op. 22

.... page 56

Sonata No. 12 in A-flat Major (Grande Sonate), Op. 26

.... page 90

Sonata No. 13 in E-flat Major (Sonata quasi una fantasia), Op. 27, No. 1

.. page 116

Sonata No. 14 in C-sharp Minor (Sonata quasi una fantasia), Op. 27, No. 2

... page 139

Sonata No. 15 in D Major (Grande Sonate), Op. 28

... page 162

Piano Sonatas VOLUME II
Edited by Stewart Gordon

Contents

About This Edition 4

Beethoven at the Turn of the 19th Century 5

Beethoven and the Piano. 6

Articulation, Dynamics and Accents, and Ornamentation in Beethoven's Music 7

    Articulation 8

    Dynamics and Accents 9

    Ornamentation 9

Tempo and Pulse in Beethoven's Music 10

    Metronome Markings for Beethoven's Sonatas in This Volume 12

About the Op. 14 Set. 13

    Sonata No. 9 in E Major, Op. 14, No. 1. 16

    Sonata No. 10 in G Major, Op. 14, No. 2 33

About Op. 22 54

    Sonata No. 11 in B-flat Major (Grande Sonate), Op. 22 56

About Op. 26 87

    Sonata No. 12 in A-flat Major (Grande Sonate), Op. 26 90

About the Op. 27 Set. 113

    Sonata No. 13 in E-flat Major (Sonata quasi una fantasia), Op. 27, No. 1 116

    Sonata No. 14 in C-sharp Minor (Sonata quasi una fantasia), Op. 27, No. 2 139

About Op. 28 160

    Sonata No. 15 in D Major (Grande Sonate), Op. 28 162

About This Edition

Ludwig van Beethoven (1770–1827) is often regarded as a link between the balance and clarity of Classicism and the emotional intensity and freedom of Romanticism. In the 32 piano sonatas he experimented constantly with structure and content. These works span a period of almost 30 years of Beethoven's mature creative life. He used the sonatas as a workshop in which to try out innovations, many of his compositional techniques appearing in the sonatas first and then later in chamber or symphonic works.

Of the sonatas in this volume, autographs exist for Op. 26, Op. 27, No. 2 (the first and final pages are missing), and the Op. 28. All of the sonatas were published shortly after they were written. This edition is based on the existing autographs and the first editions, published by various Viennese engravers. In addition, a number of other esteemed editions were referenced when decisions have had to be made due to lack of clarity or inconsistency in the first edition, or when realization of ornamentation was open to question. Editors that have been referenced are (in alphabetical order): d'Albert,[1] Arrau,[2] Bülow,[3] Casella,[4] Craxton/Tovey,[5] Geoffroy,[6] Köhler/Ruthardt,[7] Krebs,[8] Martienssen,[9] Schenker,[10] Schnabel,[11] and Wallner.[12] In the context of the footnotes, the editions with more than one contributing editor are referenced in an abbreviated manner, using only the last name of either the first editor or the more prominent editor. Recommended solutions to problems are suggested in this edition. If, however, a problem is such that it is open to several solutions, other editors' conclusions are also often included in the footnotes. In this way students and their teachers are not only offered choices in individual cases but, more importantly, gain an awareness of the editorial and performance problems that attend studying and playing this music.

The insurmountable problems that arise in trying to distinguish between the staccato dot and the wedge in these works have led this editor to join ranks with most others in using but one marking (dot) for both symbols. The reasons behind this decision and the exceptions to it are clarified in the essay on Articulation.

Like almost all other editors, I have chosen not to indicate pedaling markings in the sonatas. Factors such as aesthetics of the period, Beethoven's personal sense of coloration in using the pedal, the acoustical properties of the various instruments he used, the variety of pedal mechanisms he encountered, and the subtlety of the art of pedaling in itself form a network of variables that would render traditional pedal markings of little help at best and misleading at worst. Rather, the matter of pedaling, especially as might be applicable to music of this era, must be based on innumerable choices that result from stylistic awareness and careful listening, these possibility changing as different instruments or performance venues are encountered.

Both autographs and first editions contain inconsistencies. First editions especially are prone to many discrepancies, such as differences in articulation in parallel passages in expositions and recapitulations of movements in sonata-allegro form, or the many cases of an isolated note in passagework without the articulation shown for all its neighbors. Even those editors whose philosophy is to be as faithful to the composer as possible subscribe to the practice of correcting these small discrepancies without taking note of such through the addition of parentheses. This edition also subscribes to that practice to avoid cluttering the performer's pages with what would turn out to be a myriad of parenthetical changes. By the same token, this editor has proceeded with an attitude of caution and inquiry, so that such changes have been made only in the most obvious cases of error or omission. If, in the opinion of the editor, there seemed to be the slightest chance that such inconsistencies could represent conscious variation or musical intent on the part of the composer, the issue has been highlighted, either by the use of parentheses that show editorial additions or footnotes that outline discrepancies and discuss possible musical intent on the part of the composer.

Fingering in parentheses indicates alternative fingering. When a single fingering number attends a chord or two vertical notes, the number indicates the uppermost or lowermost note. Octaves on black keys are usually fingered 1-4, but it is acknowledged that such fingering may prove too much of a stretch for some hands. Thus, (4) in parenthesis indicates that players with small hands may want to substitute 1-5.

---

[1] Ludwig van Beethoven, *Sonatas for Piano*, ed. Eugen d'Albert (New York: Carl Fischer, 1981, originally published in 1902).

[2] Ludwig van Beethoven, *Sonaten für Klavier zu zwei Händen*, ed. Claudio Arrau, revised by Lothar Hoffmann-Erbrecht (Frankfurt: C. F. Peters, 1973).

[3] Ludwig van Beethoven, *Sonatas for the Piano*, ed. Hans von Bülow and Sigmund Lebert, trans. Theodore Baker (New York: G. Schirmer, 1894, currently distributed by Hal Leonard, Milwaukee).

[4] Ludwig van Beethoven, *Sonatas for Piano*, ed. Alfredo Casella (Rome: G. Ricordi, 1919).

[5] Ludwig van Beethoven, *Complete Pianoforte Sonatas*, ed. Harold Craxton, annotated Donald Francis Tovey (London: Associated Board of the Royal School of Music, 1931).

[6] Ludwig van Beethoven, *Sonatas*, ed. under the direction of Dominique Geoffroy (Paris: Editions Henry Lemoine, 1992).

[7] Ludwig van Beethoven, *Sonaten für Klavier*, ed. Louis Köhler and Adolf Ruthardt (Frankfurt: C. F. Peters, originally published in 1890).

[8] Ludwig van Beethoven, *Sonatas for Piano*, ed. Carl Krebs (Miami: Warner Bros. Publications of Kalmus Editions, originally published in 1898).

[9] Ludwig van Beethoven, *Sonaten für Klavier zu zwei Händen*, ed. Carl Adolf Martienssen (New York: C. F. Peters, 1948).

[10] Ludwig van Beethoven, *Complete Piano Sonatas*, ed. Heinrich Schenker with a new introduction by Carl Schachter (New York: Dover, 1975, originally published in 1934).

[11] Ludwig van Beethoven, *Sonatas for the Pianoforte*, ed. Artur Schnabel (New York: Simon & Schuster, 1935).

[12] Ludwig van Beethoven, *Klaviersonaten*, ed. B. A. Wallner, fingering by Conrad Hansen (Munich: G. Henle, 1952, 1980).

Ornaments such as trills, turns, and mordents are discussed in footnotes. When a single rapid appoggiatura or grace note is not footnoted, the performer should choose whether to execute it before the beat or on the beat. However, in some cases this editor indicates a preference for on-the-beat execution in the music by using a dotted line that connects the ornamental note with the base note it is to be played with. Execution of Beethoven's ornaments is addressed in more detail in the essay on Ornamentation.

Beethoven at the Turn of the 19th Century

Beethoven's reputation as a young composer-pianist was well established during the period of the sonatas in this volume (1798–1802). That segment of the Viennese aristocracy interested in the arts had accepted him into their homes, often creating opportunities for him to display his performing and creative talents. They began to support him financially, and by 1800 the composer was beginning to be involved in public concerts that benefited him both artistically and financially.

Beethoven reported some of these successes to his lifelong friend in Bonn, Franz Gerhard Wegeler (1765–1848), in a lengthy letter dated June 29, 1801. The composer wrote of his friendship with Prince Karl von Lichnowsky (ca. 1756–1814) and the fact that the Prince had awarded him a stipend of 600 gulden (estimated at an amount slightly over $2,000). During much of this period Beethoven was a live-in guest in the home of Prince Karl and his wife Christiane (1765–1841). Beethoven also wrote in his letter to Wegeler that "compositions bring me in a good deal; and I may say that I am offered more commissions than it is possible for me to carry out."[13]

Beethoven's name is linked romantically with several women during this period, all of them of the noble class: Josephine Clary and Christine Gerhardi, who had reputations as fine singers, as well as Anna Luise Barbara Keglevich (d. 1813) and his piano student Giulietta Guicciardi (1784–1856). Although these women all married into nobility, their involvement with Beethoven is a testament to the fact that he was accepted and admired in their circles.

Interestingly, many documents of the day erroneously ascribe a noble heritage to Beethoven himself by altering the *van* in his name, a part of many family names of Netherlands origins, to *von*, a signature of nobility in Germanic names. Historians have even speculated that the composer did little or nothing to correct this misapprehension.

The one ominous specter that had begun to show itself in the composer's life is his impending deafness. Beethoven complained in the aforementioned letter to Wegeler that "for the last three years my hearing has become weaker and weaker." He added that his physicians believed the condition to be linked to chronic indigestion. After describing several prescribed treatments Beethoven gave a full, heartrending account of his condition:

As a result I have been feeling, I may say, stronger and better; but my ears continue to hum and buzz day and night. I must confess that I lead a miserable life. For almost two years, I have ceased to attend any social functions, just because I find it impossible to say to people: I am deaf. If I had any other profession I might be able to cope with my infirmity; but in my profession it is a terrible handicap. And if my enemies, of whom I have a fair number, were to hear about it, what would they say? ...In order to give you some idea of this strange deafness, let me tell you that in the theater I have to place myself quite close to the orchestra in order to understand what the actor is saying, and that at a distance I cannot hear the high notes of instruments or voices. As for the spoken voice, it is surprising that some people have never noticed my deafness; but since I have always been liable to fits of absentmindedness, they attribute my hardness of hearing to that. Sometimes I can scarcely hear a person who speaks softly; I can hear sounds, it is true, but cannot make out the words. But if anyone shouts, I can't bear it! Heaven alone knows what is to become of me.

Later Beethoven wrote, "I am only telling you this as a secret." He fantasized that perhaps he would have Wegeler rent a house in the country for him, and that living the life of a peasant for six months would somehow effect a change for the better.[14] The onset of the composer's deafness continued to weigh heavily on his mind, for on July 1, 1801, he wrote to his violinist friend, Karl Amenda (1771–1836), who lived in Courland, "Let me tell you that my most prized possession, my *hearing*, has greatly deteriorated. When you were still with me, I already felt the symptoms; but I said nothing about them. Now they have become much worse."[15] Beethoven wrote again to Wegeler the following November 16th, "But so far my hearing is not a bit better; and I am inclined to think, although I do not dare to say so definitely, that it is a little weaker."[16]

Thus, during this period Beethoven's professional success and his romantic aspirations were offset by his awareness of the infirmity that was to take from him completely his most "prized possession" and test his spirit to the limit.

---

[13] *The Letters of Beethoven*; vol. I, ed. and trans. Emily Anderson (London: St. Martin's Press, 1961), p. 51.
[14] Ibid., p. 58.
[15] Ibid., p. 63.
[16] Ibid., p. 66.

Beethoven and the Piano

The piano was undergoing both structural and aesthetic change during the four decades that encompass Beethoven's creative life. Thus, the composer's use of the instrument reflected not only the piano's growing strength and flexibility, but also his vision as to the direction in which the piano was headed and the possibilities for its future. In his composing Beethoven pushed the capabilities of the pianos to the limit, frequently expressing dissatisfaction in his letters with the overall limitations of the piano in general. This feeling of frustration led him to conceive music that even today exploits the strengths of the fully developed piano, an instrument that did not emerge until the mid-19th century, well after Beethoven's death.

On the other hand, awareness of the properties of the various pianos that figured prominently in Beethoven's life can teach us much about the reality of his musical world; to a certain extent he could not escape being influenced and limited by the instruments he actually used. Beethoven's correspondence suggests that, between his arrival in Vienna in late 1792 and 1803, the composer did not own a piano, but rather probably made use of pianos loaned to him by various makers who were eager to gain his endorsement. Moreover, Beethoven's choice was wide, for there were more than 100 keyboard instrument-makers in the city of Vienna by about 1800. Notwithstanding this array, several instruments are associated closely with Beethoven during this period.

The first of these are pianos made by Andreas Stein (1728–1792). Beethoven, like Wolfgang Amadeus Mozart (1756–1791), visited Stein at his place of work in Augsburg, Beethoven's visit taking place in 1787. After Stein's death the business was taken over by his children, Matthäus Andreas (1776–1842) and Nannette (n.d.). In 1802 Nannette married a Viennese pianist who had worked with Stein, Andreas Streicher (1761–1833), and with her husband began to build pianos independently in Vienna. Beethoven maintained a close, life-long friendship with the Streichers, sustaining a lively correspondence with Nannette, albeit mostly about domestic matters, such as the hiring of reliable household servants, recommendations for good tailors and the like. However, Beethoven wrote a letter in late 1796 to Andreas which praises an instrument sent to him as "an excellent instrument." Although this instrument is not specified by name, it was probably a Stein, since the Streichers did not use their own name on pianos until around 1810. In the letter Beethoven comments that the piano may be "too good"[17] for him inasmuch as he didn't have to work hard enough to produce a beautiful, singing line. Is this comment born of the composer's individual brand of humor or does it hold a veiled complaint? That answer will never be known for sure.

Two other piano-makers are also believed to have built instruments well-known to Beethoven: Franz Jakob Späth (1714–1786) of Regensburg and Anton Walter (1752–1826) of Vienna. Beethoven shared with Mozart the view that Späth pianos were not as good as those made by the Stein-Streicher families. Carl Czerny (1791–1857), who later became Vienna's leading piano teacher and history's most celebrated composer of exercise pieces designed to develop technique, reported that a Walter was in Beethoven's home in 1801 when, as a boy of 10, Carl first auditioned for the composer. Czerny described the Walter as "the best one made then."[18]

Although it is believed that Beethoven was familiar with and probably used instruments made by these makers, there are no specific, extant instruments preserved in museums that can be linked directly to the composer in this early period. Furthermore, caution must be used in assuming that those instruments that are extant represent in exact detail the pianos Beethoven used, for piano makers were quick both to try experimental models and to customize instruments for individuals.

Still, the pianos made by all of the aforementioned piano makers could be categorized as German or Austrian and as such shared certain general characteristics, which, in the minds of Beethoven and his contemporaries, formed a marked contrast with those made in England at about the same time. Many contemporary accounts refer to this difference. For example, Johann Nepomuk Hummel (1778–1837) in the English edition (1829) of his extensive method book for pianists, *A Complete Theoretical and Practical Course of Instructions on the Art of Playing the Piano Forte…*, writes that the German piano "may be played upon by the weakest hand," allowing the performer "every possible degree of light and shade, … speaks clearly and promptly," and "has a round, fluty tone." By contrast, according to Hummel, the English pianos "do not admit the same facility of execution as the German; the touch is heavier; the key sinks much deeper; and, consequently, the return of the hammer upon the repetition of a note cannot take place so quickly." Hummel praises the English pianos, however, for "durability and fullness of tone," and describes melodies played on them as having "peculiar charm and harmonious sweetness."[19]

Similarly, Friederich Kalkbrenner (1785–1849), the celebrated French pianist, teacher and composer who in 1831 befriended Chopin upon the young Polish composer's arrival in Paris, comments in his *Méthode pour apprendre le piano-forte a l'aide du guide mains*, Op. 108 (Paris: J. Miessonnier Fils, 1831) that Viennese pianos are "extremely easy to play," resulting in piano playing noted for "precision, clarity, and rapidity of execution." English pianos, according to Kalkbrenner, "have a fuller sound and a heavier keyboard action," resulting in playing of "larger style and a beautiful way of singing."[20]

---

[17] The passage is from a letter dated November 19, 1796, and is quoted by William S. Newman in *Beethoven on Beethoven: Playing His Piano Music His Way* (New York: W. W. Norton, 1988), p. 50.

[18] William S. Newman, "Beethoven's Pianos Versus His Piano Ideals," *Journal of the American Musicological Society*, XXIII/3 (Fall, 1970): p. 484.

[19] Johann Nepomuk Hummel, *A Complete Theoretical and Practical Course of Instructions on the Art of Playing the Piano Forte, Commencing with the Simplest Elementary Principles and Including Every Information Requisite to the Most Finished Style of Performance* (London: T. Boosey & Co., 1829), pp. 64–65.

[20] The passage is quoted by William Leslie Sumner in *The Pianoforte* (London: MacDonald & Co., 1966), p. 49.

These subjective comments reflect some specific differences in construction between the two schools of piano building. Typically, the diameter of the strings in the English pianos was about 50% greater. There were three strings per note in the English, but only two in German-Austrian. English soundboards were thicker and slightly convex; German-Austrian were lighter and flat. The hammers were larger and heavier in most English models, which partially accounts for more resistant action. Dampers, on the other hand, were heavier and reportedly more reliable in the German-Austrian models. One other significant difference was that of the pedal mechanism. Knee pedals were generally used in the German-Austrian models, often one for each knee, controlling the right and left halves of the keyboard. Foot pedals were typical of the English. Although ranges differed slightly from model to model during this period, the standard was between five and one-half and six octaves, and it has been observed by noted American pianist and musicologist William S. Newman (1912–2000) that, save for one exception in the Op. 14, No. 2, the first 20 sonatas, up to Op. 53, do not exceed the five octaves from F̲ to f'''.[21]

Thus, one can assume that Beethoven worked with the German-Austrian pianos almost exclusively until 1803, when the French piano manufacturer Sébastien Érard (1752–1831) presented him with an Érard piano as a surprise gift. Subsequently, Beethoven received an English Broadwood in 1818 and a Viennese Graf in 1825, a piano especially designed to cope with Beethoven's deafness. Consideration of the characteristics of these later instruments and the possibilities they presented to the composer will take place in conjunction with the study of sonatas that emanate from those periods. Even so, Beethoven's letters and related documents suggest that he retained a fondness for German-Austrian pianos, especially those built by the Stein-Streicher families, throughout his career.

In translating this information into a working aesthetic for studying and performing the sonatas, pianists must take into account on one hand the qualities of the German-Austrian piano of the period and, on the other, simulate Beethoven's musical concepts, including those that push such instruments to, and even beyond, their existing limitations. Thus, one begins to understand how the light actions of the German-Austrian pianos made playing the left-hand arpeggiation of the *Prestissimo* of the Op. 2, No. 1 or the tremolos of the opening movement of the Op. 13 fun rather than problematic. Similarly, one can try to simulate the sweet, somewhat thin tone that made for deft, light execution of ornamented lines, such as those found in the second movements of the Op. 2, No. 1 or the Op. 10, No. 1. By the same token, scholars can conjecture that Beethoven's vision as to the future strength and sonority of the piano must have contributed to his concept of the opening chords of the Op. 13 or the profound gloom of the coda of the *Largo e mesto* of the Op. 10, No. 3. Weighing and balancing these diverse influences contribute significantly to the ever-fascinating challenges that confront the pianist in attempting to recreate and communicate the essence of this marvelous music.

Articulation, Dynamics and Accents, and Ornamentation in Beethoven's Music

Performers always seek definitive answers with regard to matters of articulation and ornamentation, for they like to feel secure in the knowledge that they are realizing the composer's intentions accurately. Unfortunately, Beethoven research has not been able to provide such answers for many textural problems, and it is very possible that solutions to the problems that attend research in this area will never be forthcoming. There are several reasons for this state of affairs.

There exist autographs of only 13 of the sonatas. One would assume that these manuscripts could provide evidence of Beethoven's intentions for the particular sonatas represented and by logically applying principles gleaned from study of these pages to other sonatas arrive at definite answers for performance problems. Unfortunately, such is not the case, for the autographs are often hastily written and extremely messy, so that some portions are virtually indecipherable and many pages seem riddled with apparent inconsistencies.

Beethoven's autograph of Sonata No. 32 in C Minor, *Op. 111, second movement, measures 106–117*

---

[21] William S. Newman, *Performance Practices in Beethoven's Piano Sonatas* (New York: W. W. Norton, 1971), p. 38.

Scholars are confronted with a paradox. On one hand, Beethoven was a composer who was very particular about the details of his music, according to contemporary evidence such as personal letters, conversation books, and reminiscences of those who knew him. On the other hand, he leaves behind a legacy of manuscripts that are far from clear. This paradox has resulted in a veritable army of scholars throughout the 19th and 20th centuries attempting to unscramble the autographs and fathom the exact desires of the composer. Such research continues to this day but, notwithstanding its good intentions, answers to many questions remain elusive and, indeed, scholars have not always arrived at the same conclusions.

Similarly, research has been lavished on the first, or early, published editions of Beethoven's works. Two problems arise in examining these printed documents. First, engravers make mistakes and these editions, like all editions, are subject to error. Indeed, Beethoven complains in his letters about errors in published works; in one case, that of the Nägeli publication of the Op. 31 set of piano sonatas, the composer was so upset that he requested the edition be withdrawn. Secondly, printing technology of the time was not refined to a point that even a careful reader can be sure of all details. This is particularly true in the piano sonatas when one tries to determine exactly where slurs begin and end, or what kind of a staccato marking attends many of the notes.

Notwithstanding these difficulties, each generation of musicians continues to study these sources of this music in an attempt to glean as much guidance as possible with regard to how it should be performed. In this edition an attempt has been made not only to present the editor's solutions to specific problems as they arise, but also to indicate choices in instances where scholars have differed with one another.

Articulation

Dots and Wedges: When Beethoven proofread his copyist's work of both the Symphony No. 7, Op. 92 and the String Quartet, Op. 132, the composer indicated that he considered dots and wedges different types of accents. Thus, the composer notes, "Where there is a dot above a note, a wedge must not be put, and vice-versa," and "♩ ♩ ♩ ♩ and ♩ ♩ ♩ ♩ are not identical."[22]

Unfortunately, there is no further clarification by the composer, especially as such markings might apply to playing piano music instead of string music. The autographs, moreover, are frequently unclear in this regard, a given mark often looking like it could be either a dot or a wedge; and, when the marks are clear, they often exhibit inexplicable inconsistencies, the dots and wedges changing back and forth within the context of a single passage without apparent reason. First editions, moreover, never seem to differentiate, a dot-wedge marking that undoubtedly meant some degree of staccato appearing with many changes of shape and degrees of thickness.

---

[22] *Letters of Beethoven*, vol. III, pp. 1241–42.

As a result of this confusion, editors of Beethoven's piano music who often began their work with the hope of being able to differentiate between dots and wedges eventually come to realize that doing so means incorporating a lot of guesswork into their editions and making large numbers of changes in the name of consistency. Thus, most editors have given up making such differentiation and simply adopt one kind of marking in their editions. Consequently, only dots are to be found in the publications prepared by Arrau, Casella, Bülow, Geoffroy, Köhler, Krebs, Martienssen, Schnabel, and Wallner. This edition conforms to such a tradition. However, in those sonatas where the autograph is extant and examination of dots and wedges in given passages reveals enough clarity and logic to warrant consideration by performers, such information will be footnoted. Of the well-known 20th-century editors, only Schenker and Tovey attempt to use two types of accent, these editors of necessity relying on personal choice for a multitude of questionable cases.

Phrasing and/or Slurring: The aforementioned difficulties in deciphering Beethoven's autographs, as well as the vagaries and inconsistencies found in first editions, result in many problematic areas regarding phrasing or slurring. Every editor must face many instances in which the choice is to leave unaltered seemingly inconsistent phrasing or to "correct" such cases by applying generally accepted musical principles and/or logic. Some editors are quick to assume error and make changes. Others are more apt to leave the original in place, adopting as much clarity as possible, and let the performer decide at some point in time whether or not the inconsistency is part of the composer's intent. In this edition, the textual source has been preserved in a high percentage of these cases. Frequently the inconsistency has been pointed out to highlight the problem for the performer, particularly in those cases where well-known 20th-century editors seem to have differed markedly with each other or are at odds with the source of the text.

In addition to the difficulty of clarity and consistency, there is a problem that is part of a larger performance practice issue attending much of he music of the late-18th and early-19th centuries. It can be observed that much of this music comes to us by way of autographs or first editions with phrasing or slurring patterns that frequently stop at points that rob the phrase of a long-line concept. These points often fall at the ends of measures.

Late-19th-century musical thinking emphasized the long line, a concept that often dictates phrasing across the bar line to the next downbeat or further. When confronted by the short phrase or slurring patterns in these earlier works, 19th-century editors often adopted a practice whereby the patterns were simply changed by extending them to conform with long-line musical thinking. If questions were raised about taking this liberty, two arguments were usually put forward: the short phrase-slur marks were carryovers from a standard practice used in writing bowing for strings; and printing conventions and/or limitations of the period dictated ending phrases or slurring at the bar line.

In the mid-20th century scholars began to revisit this issue and to consider the possibility that perhaps these markings could not be dismissed quite so easily. Questions were raised that seemed to challenge traditional rationale. First, why would so many masters who were skilled keyboard players confuse keyboard techniques with string bowing to the extent of inserting bowing markings into their keyboard music, rather than markings that would assist the keyboard player? Second, how can one ascribe to period printing practice limitations that cursory observation proves did not exist? In other words, one can find many examples in early printed music where phrasing or slurring extends over the bar line, sometimes for several measures, sometimes stopping in the middle of measures. Finally, it should be noted that much slurring is not addressed by considerations of articulation vis–a–vis the bar line (for example, the frequently encountered two-note slurs in Beethoven).

Such speculation invites us to consider that perhaps much of the articulation was born of a touch sensitivity that came directly out of playing earlier keyboard instruments, such as the harpsichord and the fortepiano. In playing these instruments sustaining sound was not as important a consideration as it later became, since instruments of the time were limited in this regard. By the same token, refinement in executing individual note values and shorter phrase groups was more important as an expressive device. This focus led to a sensitivity of touch that allowed for the projection of various articulated groupings without destroying the longer musical thought, a sensitivity that was enhanced by the light action of the keyboards themselves. If today's keyboardists begin to look at the original phrase groups in this light, they will discover that it is quite possible to develop fingertip sensitivity to an extent that would permit honoring all of Beethoven's slurring with meticulous accuracy without impairing the longer musical thought.

Dynamics and Accents

Beethoven often repeats dynamic markings within the context of the same passage as a means of suggesting musical emphasis beyond the level of intensity directed by the dynamic itself. Since Beethoven was writing for the early piano, these duplicated dynamic markings do not serve the function of indicating which manual of a two-manual instrument each hand is to play upon. In recent editions that adapt such early keyboard music for the piano, many editors preserve only one of the duplicated dynamic indications.

To the contrary, Beethoven's repetition of dynamic marks seems to be a gesture meant to elicit a greater degree of emotional response on the part of the performer. As the player views and studies the music, the exhortation again and again to play *forte*, for example, is much the same as the emphatic gesture a conductor might use to incite ensemble musicians to more intense playing. Similarly, repeated reminders to play softly invites the performer to settle in to a mode of performance that effectively communicates the appropriate mood, be it one of tenderness, thoughtful contemplation, or prayerful meditation. Accordingly, Beethoven's dynamic repetitions are preserved by most editors, as they have been in this edition.

Beethoven uses a variety of markings to indicate accent: *sforzando*, *forte-piano* (or *fortissimo-piano*), *subito forte* (or *fortissimo*), *subito piano* (or *pianissimo*), wedges (vertical and horizontal), as well as the implied accent of *rinsforzando*, instituted by a re-enforced touch. In addition, certain ornaments invite accents, such as the initial note of a rapid mordent placed over the first note of a two-note slur (*Schneller*). Some form of such accent will be encountered by the performer in every movement of these sonatas, almost on every page. Thus, it becomes apparent that accents were of great importance to Beethoven, and meticulous realization of them is absolutely necessary for stylistic performance of this music.

Notwithstanding the importance of accents, there is much about their details of execution that remains elusive. Scholars have attempted without much success to discern a pattern of consistency in Beethoven's indications that would help determine how much accent is appropriate for a given symbol or in a given context. Although there has been a considerable amount of speculation and some attempts to codify Beethoven's symbols, no definitive guide has emerged and garnered widespread acceptance. Hence, exact interpretation and refinement of execution must be left to the performer. This responsibility, moreover, can be one of considerable complexity, for Beethoven uses accents in conjunction with metric accentuation, sometimes working with the strong beats of the meter, sometimes contrary to them (syncopation). In addition, the composer constantly employs elements of surprise in his music, suddenly accenting the unexpected or changing dynamic levels rapidly without warning. Studying these accents and arriving at a convincing execution of them are among the challenges that give Beethoven's music both its excitement and enduring vitality.

Ornamentation

Evidence exists that Beethoven was well acquainted with the 18th-century tradition of ornamentation that his generation inherited. Such a tradition is documented most clearly for keyboard players in the *Essay on the True Art of Playing Keyboard Instruments*[23] by Carl Philipp Emanuel Bach (1714–1788), a work published four times between the years 1753 and 1797. Czerny reported that he was asked to acquire this work when, at the age of 10, he began his lessons with Beethoven. By the same token, style in piano playing was undergoing profound change during Beethoven's lifetime and ornamentation was part of that process. By the middle of the 19th century, just a few decades after Beethoven's death, new ways of ornamentation were to be accepted as the norm by many musicians: trills beginning on the main note rather than the upper auxiliary; appoggiaturas and arpeggiation coming before the beat instead of on it; and ornamental flourishes of all kinds being written in ways that were increasingly exact and left less to the discretion of the performer.

---

[23] Carl Philipp Emanuel Bach, *Essay on the True Art of Playing Keyboard Instruments*, trans. and ed. William J. Mitchell (New York: W. W. Norton, 1949).

Beethoven lived during the first echelon of this change. For example, in his friend Johann Nepomuk Hummel's *A Complete Theoretical and Practical Course of Instruction in the Art of Playing the Pianoforte...*, published in London and in Germany at about the time of Beethoven's death (1827), it is recommended that the trill start on the main note rather than the upper auxiliary.[24] To what extent Beethoven may have been influenced by Hummel's preference in this regard is unknown, as is whether or not Hummel was reflecting a practice that had become widespread by the time this method book was published. To these speculations must be added that Beethoven was, in fact, an innovator with regard to compositional techniques, forward looking and experimental. It stands to reason that, as a pianist, he would be as inventive and adventuresome in the performance of music, especially his own, and that he was probably not given much to letting tradition stand in the way of expression.

The journey of inquiry in this area is strewn with may attempts to find definitive answers to questions regarding the realization of ornaments. Among the many notable historic quests to solve the riddle of Beethoven ornamentation are those of Franz Kullak (1844–1913) in the book *Beethoven's Piano Playing, with an Essay on the Execution of the Trill*[25] (1881) and the Beethoven section of Edward Dannreuther's (1844–1905) two-volume work entitled *Musical Ornamentation*[26] (1893–95). Simultaneous with such research efforts was the building of a performance tradition in the hands of pianists who were great Beethoven specialists, such as Artur Schnabel (1882–1951). One can even point to a teacher-pupil lineage that moved from Beethoven to Czerny, from Czerny to Theodor Leschetizky (1830–1915), and from Leschetizky to a multitude 20th-century performers, including Schnabel. Much of the time the traditions built by famous performers favored 19th-century execution of ornaments notwithstanding the cautions tendered by researchers.

Such contradictory evidence should not be regarded as a license to avoid coming to grips with the problems. Some editors have realized ornamentation with strong allegiance to contemporary principles as set forth by C.P.E. Bach. These editors do not proceed very far, however, without encountering ornamentation for which exception to the contemporary practice seems to offer solutions that are more satisfying musically and/or more practical technically. Other editors adhere to some 19th-century performance traditions without apology. Still others offer suggestions for independent evaluation on the part of the performer. For example, William S. Newman in his excellent book *Performance Practices in Beethoven's Piano Sonatas*[27] (1971) suggests that the performer must decide how to execute each trill, taking into account harmony, melody, technical fluency, and rhythm. For this edition an attempt has been made to incorporate something of all of these approaches. Thus, a realization for an ornamentation problem is always offered, but this edition also often takes note of differing viewpoints, particularly in those cases where 18th-century performance practice and a later performing tradition diverge.

To summarize, the conclusion is inescapable that there are not always definitive answers to performance problems encountered in matters of articulation and ornamentation in the Beethoven sonatas. Each generation of performers, however, needs to address these issues anew, for continuing research engages us in an ongoing concentration on the details and values of the music. Such focus gives rise to personal conviction in playing the music, even in regard to the unfathomable, and creates a resurgence of vitality for present-day performance.

Tempo and Pulse in Beethoven's Music

Beethoven provided only general tempo directions in Italian or German at appropriate points in the score. In later works he refined these directions, in some instances by adding additional descriptive phrases. There is but a single exception to this practice, that being the metronome markings Beethoven left for the Op.106. This set of indications has been problematic, however, both for playing the Op. 106 itself and for providing a key with which to sense the composer's intentions regarding tempo in general, for the markings have been deemed by most musicians to be excessively fast. William S. Newman has even gone so far as to suggest that Beethoven's hearing loss had caused him to lose touch with the reality of physical execution as well as sound at that point in life.[28] Artur Schnabel's attempt to realize these metronome markings in a recording of the Op. 106 (ca. 1930) was well intentioned, to be sure, but the breathless, often scrambled impression the performance conveys has only served to support the contention that the indications are, indeed, much too fast for comfort and clarity.

---

[24] Johann Nepomuk Hummel, *Ausführlich theoretisch-practische Anweisung zum Piano-forte Spiel*, ca. 1822–25, second edition (Vienna: Tobias Haslinger, 1828), p. 394.
[25] Franz Kullak, *Beethoven's Piano Playing, with an Essay on the Execution of the Trill*, trans. Theodore Baker (New York: G. Schirmer, 1901).
[26] Edward Dannreuther, *Musical Ornamentation*. 2 volumes (London: Novello & Co., 1893–95).
[27] Newman, Op. cit., p. 52.

[28] Ibid., p. 52.

*Ludwig van Beethoven, miniature on ivory by Christian Horneman, 1802
Beethoven-Haus, Bonn, Collection H. C. Bodmer*

Notwithstanding the limited directions from the composer himself, tempo and appropriate handling of pulse in performing Beethoven have been matters of both concern and debate from the earliest generation of scholars and performers to those of the present time. One of the most frequently cited sources on these subjects is Beethoven's early biographer Anton Schindler (1795–1864), who met the composer in 1814 and subsequently became his secretary and household assistant, intermittently until the composer's death in 1827. Schindler's biography of Beethoven underscores the composer's concern with tempo and describes Beethoven's performances of his own music in ways that suggest considerable latitude in both tempo and pulse regularity. For example, the 1840 edition of Schindler's biography of Beethoven contains a detailed account of the composer's performances of the two sonatas of Op. 14. The account focuses mostly on describing tempo changes and concludes that "…in every moment Beethoven varied the tempo as the feelings changed."[29] Performers cannot, however, put too much credence in Schindler's descriptions, for he wrote them more than a decade after Beethoven's death. Moreover, Schindler's credibility and accuracy were seriously challenged even by his contemporaries, so much so that Schindler deleted most of the commentary on Beethoven's use of tempo and pulse from the final (third) edition of his Beethoven biography (1860).

Of the many 19th-century editions of the sonatas, the best-known ones that offer metronome markings are those of Czerny and Ignaz Moscheles (1794–1870). Czerny's markings appeared twice, first in an 1842 publication, then later in 1850, the later marks almost always faster, too fast in the opinions of many musicians. Later well-known editions that include metronome markings are those by Hans von Bülow (1830–1894), Artur Schnabel, and Alfredo Casella (1883–1947). Schnabel goes a step further by indicating changes in tempi within movements, reflecting his own interpretation and possibly Schindler's perception of Beethoven's performances. Schnabel's daring in this regard has, however, engendered considerable controversy among other pianists, many taking issue with not only the individual markings, but also the concept of suggesting fluctuations within movements. Many feel that, although it is possible that Schnabel's markings worked well for him, forging basic tempi and tempo fluctuations is a process that each individual must undertake during the process of performance preparation.

Moreover, recent thinking has become somewhat sophisticated regarding selecting tempi and suggests the tempo of a given performance may be influenced by a number of variables, including the sound of the performance instrument, the surrounding acoustics, and the sensibilities of the individual performer. Thus, it is not surprising that most recent editions eschew assigning metronome markings to the sonatas. Both setting basic tempi and effecting the subtle alterations of tempo in response to the flow of the music are dependent upon many elusive factors, not the least of which is the ability of the performer to project an individual point of view convincingly.

As a point of information, a sampling of metronome markings suggested by other editors has been provided in the following table. The editorial policy of this edition, however, will align itself the majority of recent critical editions by simply presenting Beethoven's tempo directions without elaboration, imprecise as those may be.

---

[29] Anton Felix Schindler, *Beethoven As I Knew Him*, vol. II, trans. Ignaz Moscheles (London: Henry Colburn, 1840), pp. 131–40. This account is also quoted by Harold Schonberg in *The Great Pianists* (New York: Simon & Schuster, 1963), pp. 79–84.

Metronome Markings for Beethoven's Sonatas in This Volume

	Note Value	Casella	Czerny		Moscheles	Bülow	Schnabel
			1842	1850			
Op. 14, No. 1							
Allegro	♩ =	152–160	132	144	152	138	126
Allegretto	♩. =	72–76	69	72	72	60	50
Allegro commodo	♩ =	92–96	-	96	80	76	80
Op. 14, No. 2							
Allegro	♩ =	92–96	80	80	80	84	104
Andante	♩ =	88–92	116	112	96	76	72
Allegro assai	♩. =	92–96	80	88	88	76	88
Op. 22							
Allegro con brio	♩ =	84–88	76	84	84	69	80–84
Adagio con molta espressione	♪ =	104	100	116	116	100	84
Minuetto	♩ =	112	120	126	126	104	100
Allegretto	♩ =	76–80	69	76	76	63	80–84
Op. 26							
Andante con Variazioni (theme)	♪ =	76	76	80	80	80	63–66
Var. I	♪ =	-	-	88	88	88	-
Var. II	♪ =	88	92	100	104	96	88
Var. III	♪ =	-	76	92	92	80	63–66
Var. IV	♪ =	-	92	100	100	92	84
Var. V	♪ =	-	76	80	80	88	63–66
Allegro molto	♩. =	100	92	88	88	88	112
Marcia funebre	♩ =	60	72	66	60	72	52
Allegro	♩ =	138	132	120	108	116	160
Op. 27, No. 1							
Andante	♩ =	80	66	69	76	84	72
Allegro	♩. =	108–112	104	104	104	84	108
Allegro molto e vivace	♩. =	112	112	120	126	100	132
Adagio con espressione	♪ =	72	66	72	76	66	63
Allegro vivace	♩ =	138	132	132	120	126	138
Op. 27, No. 2							
Adagio sostenuto	♩ =	60	54	60	60	52	63
Allegretto	♩. =	84–88	76	80	76	56	63
Presto agitato	♩ =	92–96	80	92	92	88	88
Op. 28							
Allegro	♩. =	84	72	72	69	69	66
Andante	♪ =	88–92	84	88	104	84	84
Allegro vivace	♩. =	108	96	100	100	96	104
Allegro ma non troppo	♩. =	92	88	88	92	84	80
Più allegro quasi presto	♩. =	120	-	-	-	100	120

About the Op. 14 Set

Op. 14 title page from the first edition, reproduced by kind permission from the copy in the Austrian National Library, Hoboken Collection, S. H. Beethoven 63

The two sonatas of Op. 14 were written between 1798 and 1799 and published by Tranquillo Mollo (1767–1837), who had been a partner in the Artaria publishing firm and set up his own business in 1798. Mollo took out an ad for the Op. 14 in the *Wiener Zeitung* dated December 17, 1799. There are no autographs of either sonata, but there are sketches of all three movements of the first set, probably dating from early 1798 (not 1795 as believed earlier). These sketches were mixed in with those for the Concerto No. 2, Op. 19.

Both sonatas are dedicated to Josephine von Braun (1765–1838) whose husband Peter (1758–1819) was in charge of the two court theaters in Vienna. It was desirable and difficult for young composers to be granted performance time in one of the theaters and the dedication may have indeed paved Beethoven's way, for he was able to use the Burgtheater on the evening of April 2, 1800, for a program featuring his works.

The first of the two sonatas exists as a work for string quartet (Hess 34), Beethoven undertaking to arrange it in 1802 for a new publishing firm called Bureau d'Arts et d'Industrie. In a letter to the publisher dated July 13, 1802, the composer complained about the "unnatural mania" of transferring piano compositions to stringed instruments, but acquiesced in that case because "I was so earnestly implored to do so." The composer added the comment that "nobody else could do the same thing with ease."[30] Notwithstanding Beethoven's reluctance, the quartet arrangement was announced in the *Wiener Zeitung* a month later, on August 14, 1802, along with the Sonata No. 15 in D Major, Op. 28.

It is interesting to note that the adaptation for strings is raised a half-step, from the key of E major to F major, possibly to enable the lowest string on the 'cello to function as a dominant. Tempo markings are modified as well, the *Allegro* of the first movement being changed to *Allegro moderato* in the quartet version, and the *Allegro commodo* of the last movement to simply *Allegro*. Some editors, notably Tovey, have tried to use the patterns of accentuation in the quartet version as a guide for the piano sonata. However, the fact that the piano version preceded the quartet version by several years, as well as the composer's qualified reluctance to transfer the music to strings, would seem to make a fairly weak case for attempting to apply the string markings to the earlier piano score.

William S. Newman points to the fact that, in measure 41 of the first movement of E major sonata, Beethoven exceeds the five-octave limit ordinarily available to him on the pianos of his day. Here he wrote an F-sharp octave instead of rewriting the passage to avoid exceeding five octaves, as was his custom. This leads Newman to speculate that the note may have been available to the composer as a special feature of the Walter piano that Czerny reported to have been in the composer's home around 1801.[31]

---

[30] *Letters of Beethoven*; vol. I, pp. 74–75.
[31] William S. Newman, *Beethoven on Beethoven: Playing His Piano Music His Way* (New York: W. W. Norton, 1988), pp. 58–59.

Sonata No. 9 in E Major, Op. 14, No. 1

Autograph/facsimile:	lost
Sketches/loose pages:	movements 1, 2 and 3
First edition:	Mollo: Vienna, 1799

The first movement of the Op. 14, No. 1, marked *Allegro*, is very traditional in its use of sonata-allegro form. The first theme area extends from the opening to measure 22, where a half cadence in the dominant key ushers in the second theme. Noteworthy is the alternation between the major sixth and the minor sixth degree of the scale in measures 46–49. A closing section using the first theme starts at measure 57. The development section opens with a brief reference to the opening theme (measures 62–66), but at measure 67 the composers permits that theme to grow into a new lyrical phrase that is the focus of the development to measure 82. Here the opening theme returns as it was used at the closing of the exposition and leads to the recapitulation at measure 92. Except for a brief departure into the key of C major in measures 104–107, the recapitulation is regular. The closing theme is extended to form a short coda (measures 149–163).

The second movement is modeled on the minuet and trio concept, indeed in $\frac{3}{4}$ meter, but the composer marks it simply *Allegretto*. He undoubtedly did this to be able to effect changes from the traditional structure in the opening section. The first eight measures are repeated an octave higher. The same relationship exists between measures 17–24 and measures 25–32. Ordinarily these two sections would comprise the entire first section before the trio. However, using the main idea, the composer extends the movement from measures 33–61. The middle section, analogous to the trio, is marked *Maggiore* and it opens in C major. This section of 16 measures (63–78) is marked to be repeated and ends in the dominant. The second part of the middle section is not to be repeated (measures 79–100), opens in the dominant and recaps the opening idea at measure 89. A *da capo* is indicated, followed by a short coda (measures 101–116) based on the theme of the *Maggiore* section.

The last movement is a rondo, marked *Allegro commodo*, and its structure is that of a small **A B A C A B A** coda. The **A** section presents the opening theme in measures 1–21. The **B** section is in the dominant key (measures 21–30). The **A** section returns in measures 30–46. A lively **C** section begins in G major at measure 47 and goes to measure 83. The **A** theme returns in measures 83–98. The **B** section returns in the tonic key in measures 98–108. A final statement of **A** (measures 108–131) varies and extends the theme.

Sonata No. 10 in G Major, Op. 14, No. 2

Autograph/facsimile:	lost
Sketches/loose pages:	none
First edition:	Mollo: Vienna, 1799

The first movement is marked *Allegro* and is cast in a traditional sonata-allegro form. There is no introduction, the first theme ending at measure 25. The second theme area is in the traditional dominant (measure 26 through the downbeat of 47) and leads to a closing section with a syncopated accompaniment pattern (measures 47–63). An elaborate development first works with the opening theme of the exposition (measures 63–73). After a brief statement of the second theme in B-flat (measures 74–80), the opening theme returns with a driving triplet accompaniment (measures 81–98). Yet another section uses the opening theme (measures 98–106). A fragment possibly derived from the closing theme appears in the LH while the RH engages is scalar passagework (measures 107–114). Finally a fragment of the opening theme is accompanied by triplets once again to from a re-transition to the recapitulation (measures 115–124). The recapitulation is regular, and the movement ends with a short coda based on the opening theme (measures 187–200).

The second movement, marked *Andante*, presents a two-part theme and three variations in C major. The first part of the theme ends in the dominant in each case. The composer indicates that the second part of the theme and of the first two variations is to be repeated. The final variation is to be played without repeats and is framed by a four-measure introduction (measures 64–67) and a six-measure codetta (measures 88–93). This is the first appearance of the formal theme and variation in the context of the sonata structure. Although the set of variations presented here is modest and regular in structure, it is significant in that it heralds a marriage the composer returns to in the Opp. 26, 57, 109, and 111, the later variations assuming increased significance in the overall sonata structure.

The final movement of this work is a scherzo with a tempo of *Allegro assai*. Indeed, the spirit of the movement is one of fun and jest, but its structure, although somewhat improvisatory, resembles a rondo with the pattern **A B A C A** coda. The first statement of the opening theme is short, ending at measure 22. The **B** section is also concise (measures 23–40). When the **A** theme is presented a second time, it is extended (measures 42–72). The **C** section presents new material in C major (measures 73–124). A short re-transition uses **A** theme material (measures 124–138) and leads to a final statement of the **A** theme, extended still more (measure 138 through the downbeat of 189), and leads to a long coda based on fragments of the **A** theme (measures 189–254).

Dedicated to the Baroness von Braun

Sonata No. 9 in E Major

Ludwig van Beethoven (1770–1827)
Op. 14, No. 1

(a) According to documented performance practice of the period, the grace-note arpeggio should begin on the downbeat of measure 8. However, the RH ornament that follows on the second eighth of the measure must also be accommodated (see footnote (b)). Doing so may lead some players to feel more comfortable executing the grace notes rapidly before the downbeat, a recommended execution that also results in forceful reiteration of the B pedal point established in measure 7. This recommendation may also be applied to the recap at measure 99.

(b) The majority of the referenced editors begin this turn on the upper note, C-sharp, using four notes. Only Casella and Schnabel recommend a five-note turn starting on the main note, B. Of the six editors who write out the ornament, Bülow, Casella, Geoffroy, Schnabel, and this editor place the turn on the beat:

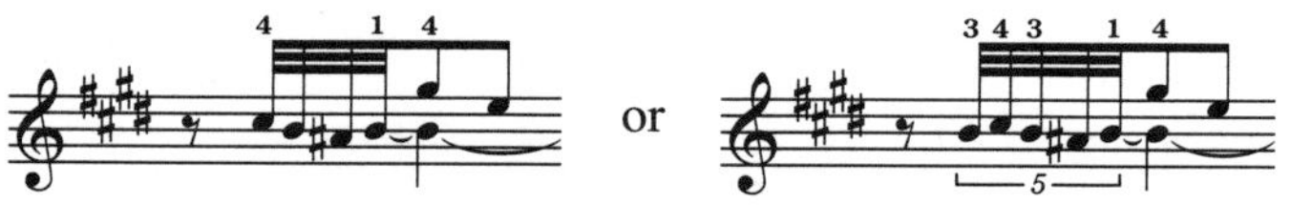

Schenker and Tovey suggest playing it before the beat, which would be consistent with strong dominant downbeats were one to play the LH arpeggiation before the beat (see footnote (a)):

These realizations can also be adapted to measure 99.

ⓒ Play the grace notes before beat 3 here and in the recapitulation at measure 118.

ⓓ The difference in touch between the second theme as presented in measures 23–24, 27–28, and the LH of measures 31–32, 35–36 is clear in the first edition—the earlier statements using portato and the later LH ones legato. The similar passage in the recapitulation (measures 115–116, 119–120 and measures 123–124, 127–128) confirms this difference. Notwithstanding this clarity, d'Albert, Bülow, Casella, and Köhler mistakenly mark all these passages *portato*. Similarly, the LH slurring in measures 31–32 and 123–124 conforms to that in the first edition, notwithstanding the fact that many editors use one slur for the two measures in each case, matching the longer slurs found in measures 35–36 and 127–128.

Moreover, both LH and RH slurring in measures 31–33 and 123–125 differ in the first edition. There is no way to determine if the differences are intentional. Although many editors alter these passages in some way to make them consistent, this editor has joined Arrau, Geoffroy, and Wallner in recreating the slurring in the first edition and letting the performer decide what, if any, adjustments need to be made.

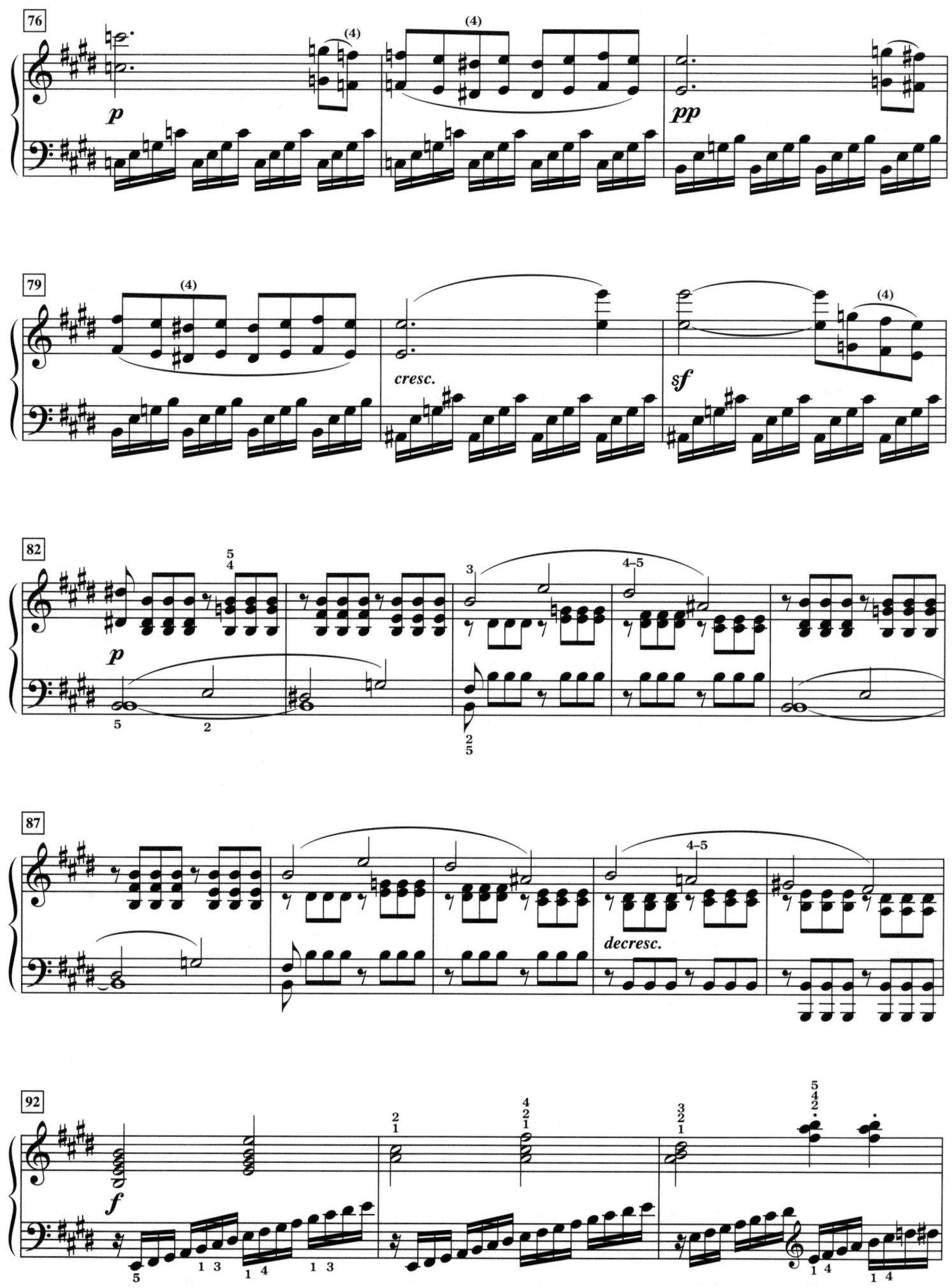

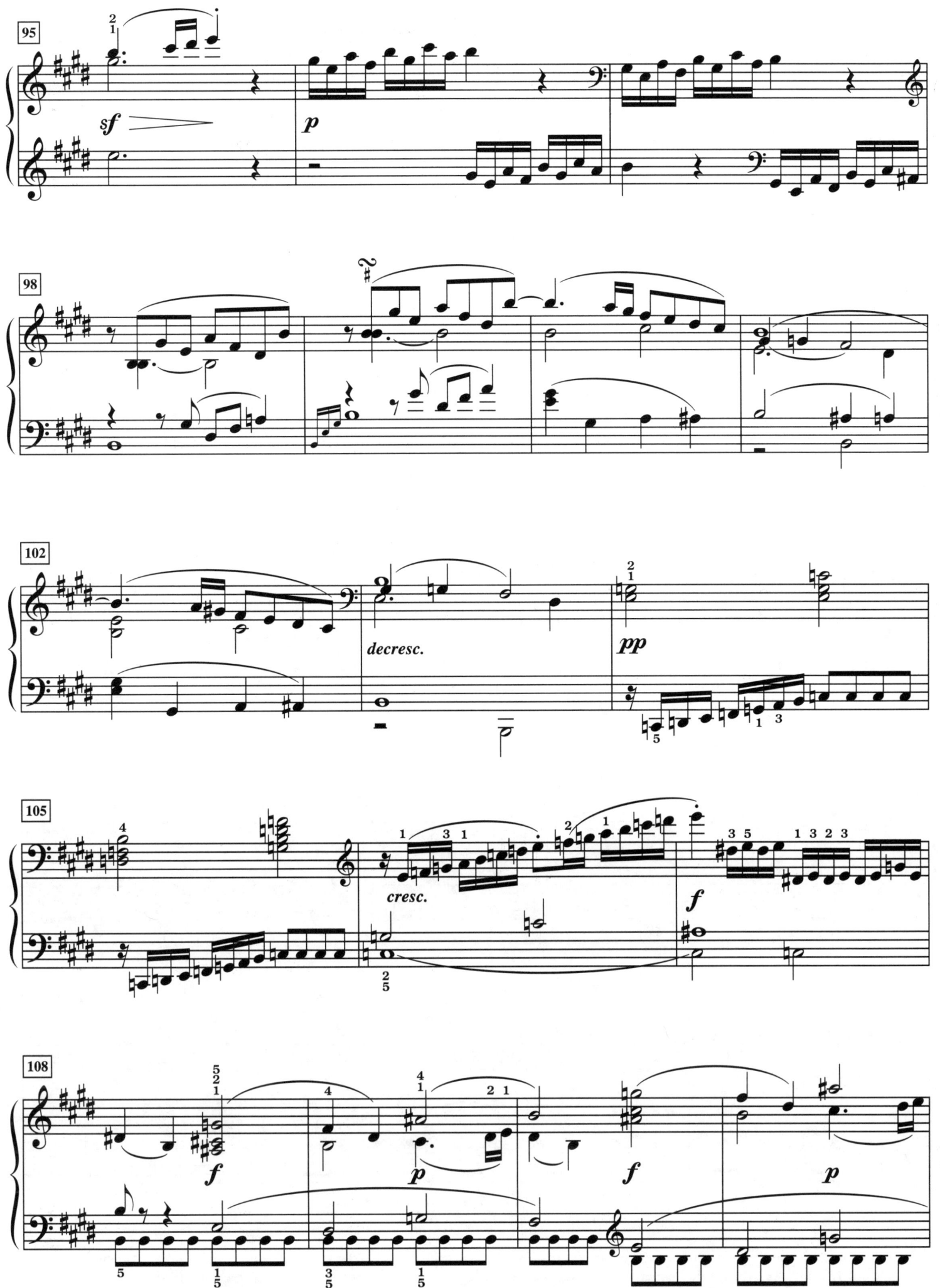

ⓕ An inconsistency in the slur mark exists in the first edition between measures 112 and 113, where the slur ends at the end of measure 112, and its exposition counterpart, measures 20 and 21, where the slur crosses the bar line to the following downbeat. Of the referenced editors, nine deem measures 112 and 113 in error and use the longer slur. Arrau, Geoffroy, and Wallner, however, reproduce the first edition's (inconsistent) markings, as does this editor.

(g) The first edition shows the single note E in the LH on the downbeats of measures 153, 154, and 155. Krebs, Schenker, and Schnabel suggest no alterations. All the other referenced editors indicate playing the octave (many showing the lower notes in parentheses), assuming its absence is due to range limitations of Beethoven's keyboard and that the composer might have preferred the more sonorous effect. This editor agrees with that assumption.

(h) For performers whose hands cannot reach over an octave, this editor recommends omitting the low E here and in measures 159–161 rather than attempting to arpeggiate this repeated chord.

ⓐ The RH middle voices are absent in the first edition. Of the referenced editors, eight suggest adding notes so that the RH part reads like that of measure 25. Arrau, Geoffroy, Martienssen, and Schnabel reproduce the measure as it appears in the first edition, Geoffroy objecting to alteration in a footnote. This editor agrees with the latter group, believing that the absence of inner voices heightens the effect of the parallel line that is taken over by the RH octave in measure 30.

ⓐ Nine of the referenced editors indicate fingering for these two trills that mandates starting on the main note, a realization with which this editor agrees:

Bülow suggests a seven-note ornament, difficult and crowded at tempo. Arrau's fingering suggests starting on the upper note in each of the trills and using a six-note figure. Apply these comments to the realization of the trills in measure 97.

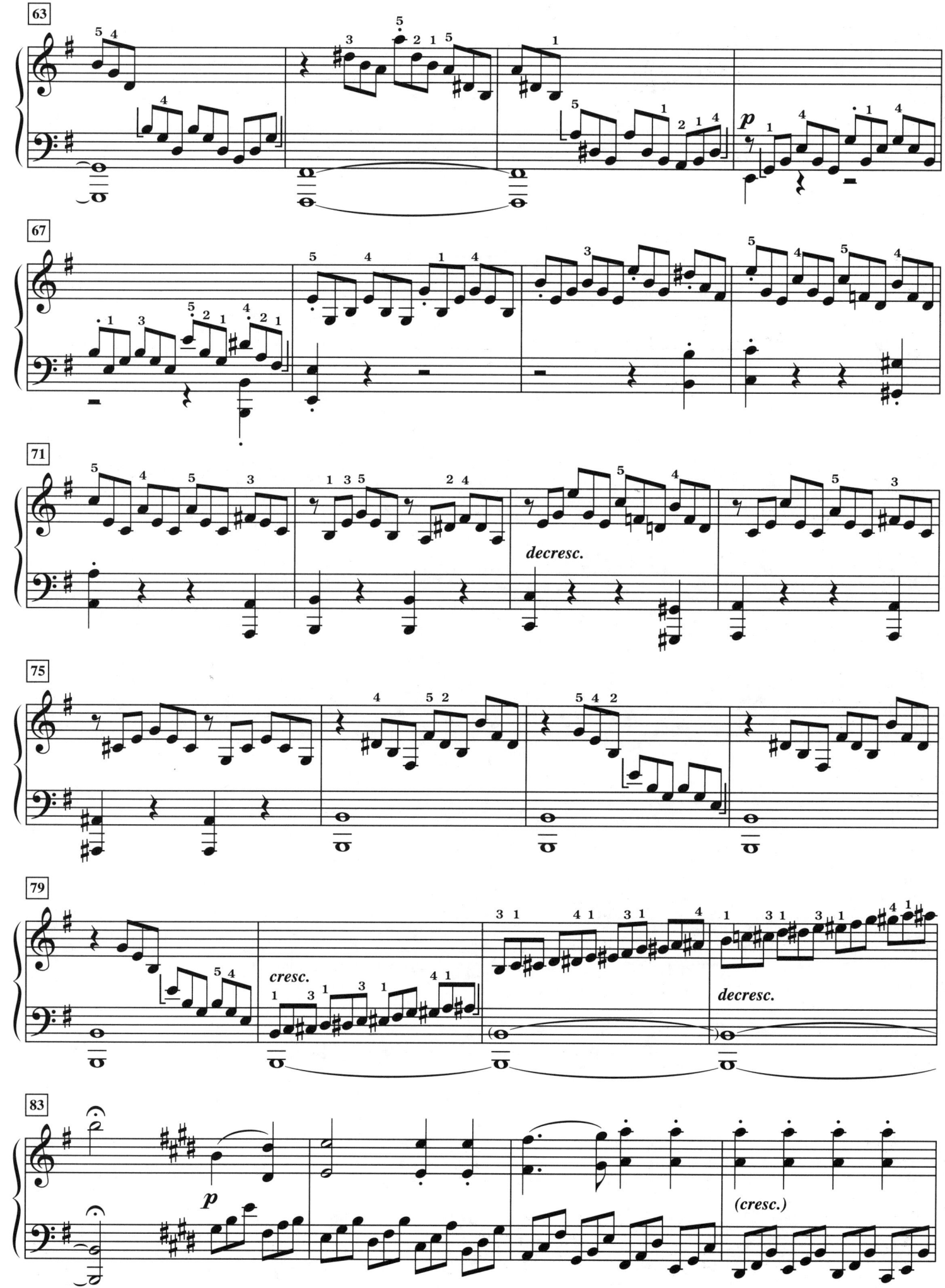

(b) Using the information cited in footnote (a), this extended trill may be realized as follows:

Dedicated to the Baroness von Braun

Sonata No. 10 in G Major

Ludwig van Beethoven (1770–1827)
Op. 14, No. 2

[Musical score: Allegro, 2/4 time, measures 1–17]

ⓐ Of the referenced editors, six indicate fingering that suggests the note on which to begin the trill. Arrau and Wallner (and this editor) prefer starting with the upper note in accordance with period practice, resulting in a six-note ornament:

Geoffroy, Köhler, Martienssen, and Schnabel show fingering that suggests starting on the main note, and Bülow writes out the ornament:

These comments can be applied to measure 133 and adapted to measure 137.

ⓑ Of the referenced editors, only four offer guidance with regard to this three-note ornament. Martienssen and Schenker suggest playing the three notes before the beat, an execution with which this editor agrees, and which preserves the series of appoggiaturas on downbeats occurring between measures 10 and 24. Bülow and Tovey regard it as the ornament C.P.E. Bach designates as a "three-toned slide" and recommend playing it on the beat, the first note being played with the first of the LH sixteenth notes. These comments can be adapted to measures 142 and 144.

ⓒ The first edition is confusing with regard to the grouping of the sixteenth notes in measures 20–24 and measures 147–151, indicating a grouping of six only at the beginning of measure 24 and strangely those sixteenths in measure 149. This indication suggests playing the sixteenth-note figures in three groups of two notes. A tradition of dividing the figures into two sets of triplets has, however, evolved. Thus, Casella suggests triplets throughout both passages, a realization that Czerny agrees with in his notes to this work. Arrau, Bülow, and Köhler recommend triplets only in measures 20, 21, and 22, and their counterparts, measures 147, 148, and 149. Geoffroy, Schenker, Tovey, and Wallner indicate sextuplets throughout both passages. This editor sides with the latter group.

ⓓ In measures 39–40, the first edition shows a dot over the first RH eighth note in measure 40, thus rendering it *portato*. Although the articulation in measures 166–167 is similar, d'Albert, Casella, Krebs, Schnabel, and Tovey tie the last note in 166 to the downbeat of 167, thus indicating that the two passages would be played with different articulation. Arrau and Köhler show ties for both. Bülow, Geoffroy, Martienssen, Schenker, and Wallner indicate playing the downbeats of measures 40 and 167 *portato*. This editor sides with the latter group.

(e) Since most Viennese pianos of the period stopped at f''', Beethoven adjusted the passagework at this point to stay within the keyboard's compass. (Compare with measure 170.) In such cases, editors often differ as to the virtue of changing the composer's solution to the range limitations of his day. In this case, the referenced editors who recommend or allow matching the two passages are Casella, Köhler, Schenker, and Tovey. If changed, the passage would read as follows:

(f) Of the referenced editors, seven offer fingering or a written-out realization that indicates how to approach the trill. Bülow, Geoffroy, Köhler, Martienssen, Schenker, and Schnabel begin on the main note. This editor likes this execution because it preserves the repeated melodic emphasis on the leading tone:

Only Arrau suggests a realization that conforms to period practice:

(g) The compass of Beethoven's piano probably limited this passage. Casella, Köhler, and Tovey suggest matching it to the passage in measure 4:

Other editors, including this one, prefer playing the passage as it was written by the composer, dealing with the limitations of his keyboard.

40

ⓐ Eight of the referenced editors provide fingering that indicates which note to start this trill. Only Arrau and this editor prefer to realize this ornament following period guidelines, beginning on the upper note. This results in a six-note ornament:

The other seven editors prefer starting on the main note, resulting in a five- or seven-note ornament:

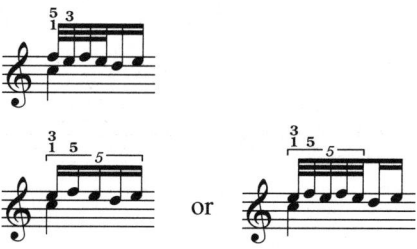

(b) The *portato* indications in this variation (measures 43–63) and the following transition (measures 64–67) appear in the first edition only in measures 43, 44, 47, 51, 55, and 64. It is logical to assume that this texture remains consistent throughout the passage, these periodic indications serving as reminders, since they often come at the beginnings of four- or eight-measure segments. Several editors add marking throughout the passage: d'Albert, Bülow, Casella, Schnabel, and Tovey.

(c) The dynamic mark *p* appears in the first edition in this measure. Eight of the referenced editors omit the marking. Geoffroy and Wallner imply by footnotes that it may be an error. Martienssen and Schenker include it without comment.

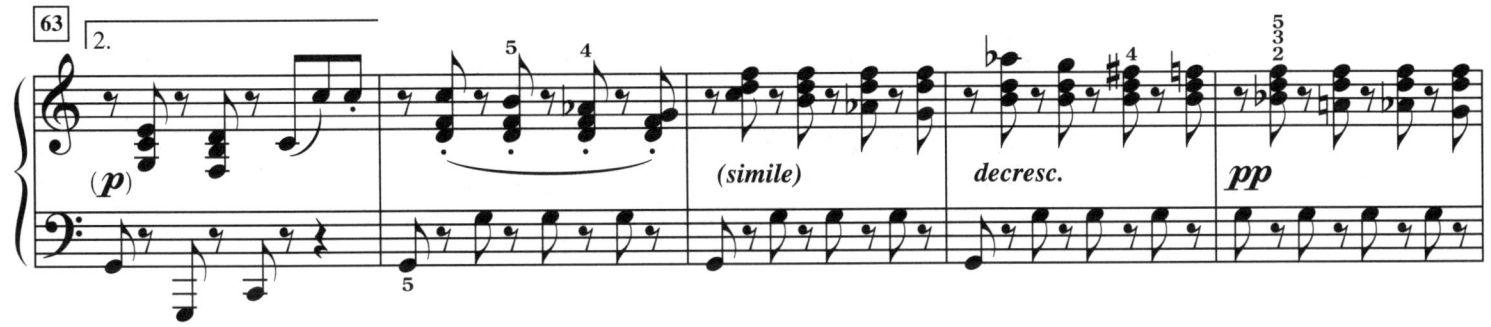

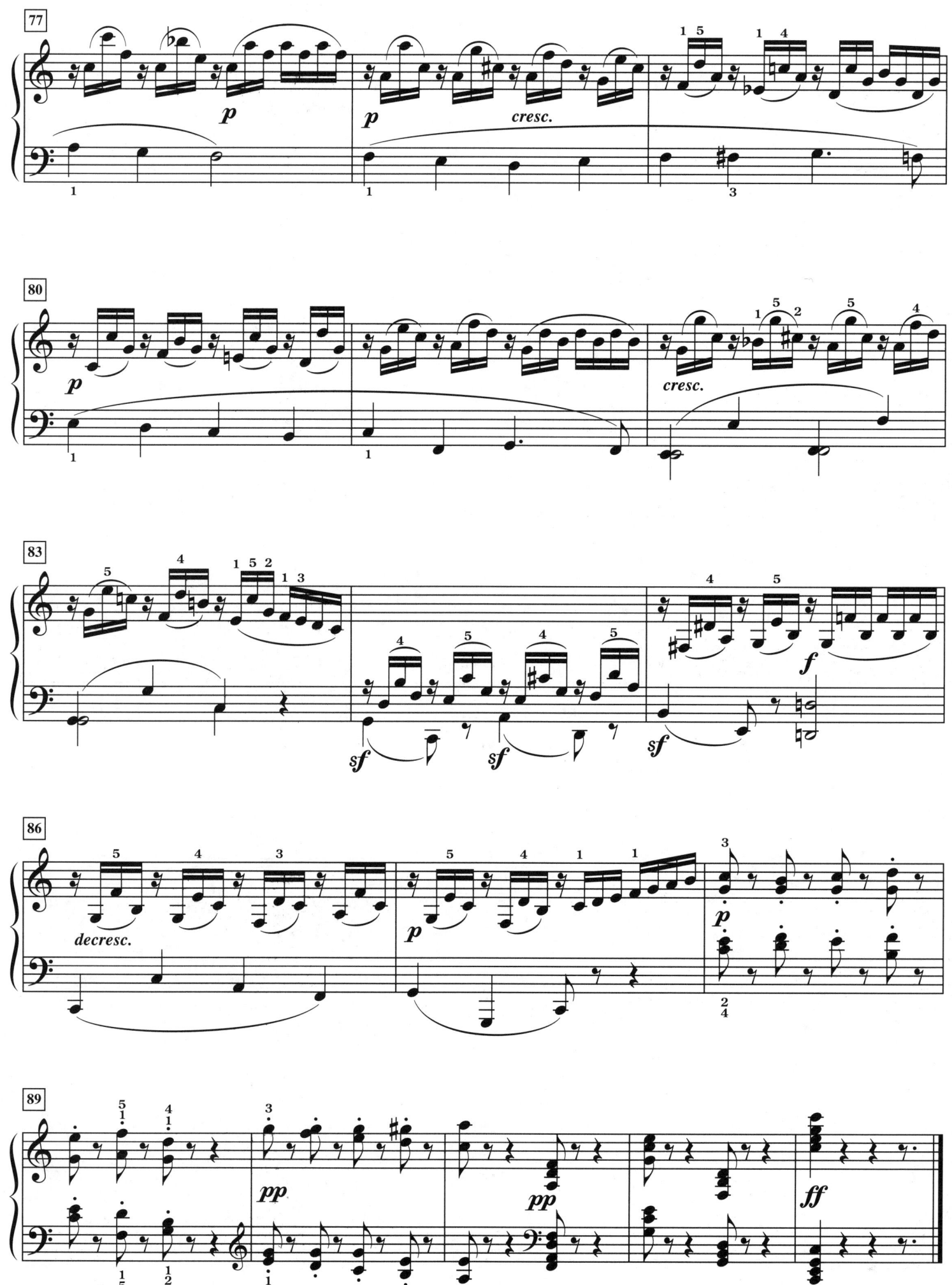

SCHERZO
Allegro assai

(a) The first edition shows the *p* markings on the downbeats of both measures 209 and 233. Eleven of the referenced editors move it to the second eighth of these measures (where the RH enters), Geoffroy and Wallner noting their departure from the first edition in a footnote. Only Casella follows the first edition (adding *subito* in both places). This editor agrees with Casella. The four-measure progression begins with the downbeats; the element of surprise is enhanced by playing the LH downbeat *p*. It seems unlikely that the engraver made the same mistake twice.

About Op. 22

Op. 22 title page from the first edition, reproduced by kind permission from the copy in the Austrian National Library, Hoboken Collection, S. H. Beethoven 117

The Op. 22 marks the composer's return to the four-movement structure that characterized the Op. 2 set, Op. 7, and Op. 10, No. 3. Thus, its concept is one of traditional classicism. In fact, many writers have observed that this work represents Beethoven's farewell to the traditional four-movement sonata of the late-18th century, for starting with the next sonata, Op. 26, the composer explores several experimental structures. In making such observation, however, one must take into account that there are still to be two relatively traditional four-movement sonatas: the Op. 28 in the usual mold, as well as the Op. 31, No. 3, with some modifications. Of the late sonatas, the Op. 101, 106, and 110 might be regarded as being cast in four movements, but all have quite unusual, experimental features.

One frequently encounters the observation that the Op. 22 is an undeservedly neglected sonata, perhaps because it does hark back to earlier concepts of structure and does not contain the dramatic gestures of sonatas such as the Op. 13. Yet, the composer thought highly of this work, evidenced by a comment in a letter to the publisher Franz Anton Hoffmeister (1754–1812) in mid-January, 1801. Hoffmeister had been active in Vienna as a publisher from about 1784. In 1800 he joined with Ambrose Kühnel (d. 1813) to found a new publishing house in Leipzig, one which Hoffmeister left in 1805 but which became part of C. F. Peters after Kühnel's death. Beethoven offered a package of compositions to the new publisher: the Septet in E-flat Major, Op. 20; Symphony No. 1 in C Major, Op. 21; the Piano Concerto No. 2 in B-flat Major, Op. 19, and the Op. 22 sonata. He refers to the sonata as a "Grand Sonata" and adds the comment, "The Sonata is first-rate (*hat sich gewaschen*)!" The composer asked for 20 ducats apiece for the works, except for the concerto, which was priced at but 10 ducats with the explanation that he did not consider it one of his best concertos.[32]

The Op. 22 is dedicated to Count Johann Georg von Browne (Browne-Camus) (1767–1827), a wealthy patron of the arts of Irish descent, who was an officer in the Imperial Russian Army at the time. Beethoven had already dedicated the String Trios, Op. 9, to the Count, describing him in the flowery dedication of that work as the "first Maecenas of his Muse." (Maecenas was a patron of Horace and Virgil in the century before Christ, and his name had come to be a symbol for any patron of the arts.) The Count is also believed to have suggested or commissioned at least two, and possibly all three, of the marches for piano duet, Op. 45. Beethoven had already dedicated the Op. 10 piano sonatas to the Count's wife, Anna Margarete, reputed to be a fine pianist.

---

[32] *Letters of Beethoven*, vol. I, pp. 47–49. (It is difficult to estimate the value of these ducats, for the coins could be made of either gold or silver.)

Sonata No. 11 in B-flat Major (Grande Sonate), Op. 22

Autograph/facsimile: lost
Sketches/loose pages: movements 1, 2, and 4
First edition: Hoffmeister: Vienna and Leipzig, 1802

The first movement, marked *Allegro con brio*, is cast in a very traditional sonata-allegro form of generous proportions. The opening theme (measures 1–21) begins with a figural motive. The second theme area begins at measure 22, presenting first a lyrical idea (to measure 44) and then brilliant passagework (measure 44 through the downbeat of 56). A closing theme (measures 56–68) begins with a lyrical phrase, making use of parallel octaves and a reference to the opening figure of the exposition. The development section opens by using the closing material of the exposition in reverse order: a reference to the opening figure, parallel octaves, and the closing theme lyrical phrase (measures 68–91). Arpeggio passages (measures 92–105) lead to a re-transition (measures 105–127) based on a combination of broken chords and the rhythm from the dotted rhythm first introduced with the closing octaves of the exposition. The recapitulation is regular and there is no coda.

The second movement (*Adagio con molta espressione*) is written in $\frac{9}{8}$ time, a signature the composer uses three times in the sonatas for second movements: here; in the Op. 31, No. 1; and in the Op. 79. The movement is in a full sonata-allegro form, complete with a development section, a structure the composer does not often use for slow movements, it appearing in only two other sonatas: the Op. 10, No. 3 and the Op. 106. The first theme in the exposition is presented in E-flat major, the key of the movement, up through measure 12. A second theme seems to begin in E-flat major at this point, and the key changes to the dominant at measure 18. The exposition ends at measure 30 and no repeat is indicated. The development (measures 31–47) uses first theme material, extending a fragment of it into sequential passagework (measures 39–47). The recapitulation is regular and there is no coda.

The third movement is marked *Minuetto*. Its structure conforms without irregularity to that of the traditional minuet and trio. The outer sections are in the key of B-flat, and the trio (*Minore*) is in the relative minor, G minor.

Similarly, the final movement, with a tempo of *Allegretto*, is cast in a very regular rondo arrangement: **A B A C A B A** coda. The opening **A** section ends at measure 18. The first departure, in the dominant, begins at the upbeat to measure 19 and modulation to the dominant is effected in measures 21–22. The first return of **A** (tonic key) is with the upbeat to measure 50. The **C** section (upbeat to measure 68–111) combines imitatively a figure used in the **B** section with new passagework, alternating the two ideas. The **A** theme returns in the tonic at measure 112 with slight variations. **B** returns in the tonic at the upbeat to measure 130. A final return of **A**, varied still more and extended, begins at the upbeat to measure 153. A coda based on the rhythmic figure of **B** begins at the upbeat to measure 183. There is a final reference to the **A** theme in the last six measures of the movement starting in measure 194.

Dedicated to the Count Johann Georg von Browne

Sonata No. 11 in B-flat Major
(Grande Sonate)

Ludwig van Beethoven (1770–1827)

Op. 22

ⓐ The first edition presents inconsistent slurring in measures 9–10 and their counterparts in the recapitulation, measures 136–137. In both hands the slurs in measure 9 end at the last sixteenth note in the measure, new slurs starting on the downbeat of measure 10. In the recapitulation, however, the RH slur does not end in measure 136, but is extended across the bar line to the downbeat of measure 137, the new slur starting on the second half of the downbeat with the first sixteenth note. The LH slur ends with the last sixteenth note of measure 136, but the new slur in 137 parallels that in the RH starting on the second half of beat 1. Of the referenced editors, only Tovey preserves this inconsistency, the rest alter all slurs to conform to the RH in measures 136–137.

ⓑ The ornaments in measures 10 and 137 are difficult at the tempo of this movement. Eight of the referenced editors indicate starting the trills on the main note either through suggested fingering or realization. Casella, Schnabel, and Tovey notate the ornament:

Bülow's idea is slightly different rhythmically:

Schnabel and Tovey also offer a facilitation this editor finds attractive:

Schnabel offers an even easier version that reduces the ornament to a grace note. D'Albert also recommends this realization:

Only Arrau insists on adhering to the performance practice represented by C.P.E. Bach. This results in a five-note trill that starts on the upper note, a solution that is extremely difficult in this context:

ⓒ The first edition shows measures 22 and 23 under a single slur. Measures 24 and 25, as well as measures 153, 154, 155, and 156, all show one-measure slurs. Editors have presented this inconsistency differently. Arrau, Geoffroy, Wallner, and this editor follow the first edition. D'Albert, Krebs, and Schnabel use single-measure slurs throughout. Casella, Köhler, Martienssen, Schenker, and Tovey slur measures in pairs throughout. Bülow uses two sets of slurs, one single over each measure, the other over pairs of measures.

ⓓ The sixths in measures 34 and 35 are marked *rf* in the first edition. All the referenced editors change the marking to *sf* to correspond with others in this thematic passage throughout the movement, a change with which this editor agrees.

ⓔ Both the original edition and a copy of this work corrected by the composer show the LH as follows:

Most of the referenced editors have changed the interval to a third, thus making it consistent with measure 174. Geoffroy, Schenker, and Wallner take note of the change, however, and Arrau follows the first edition notation without comment.

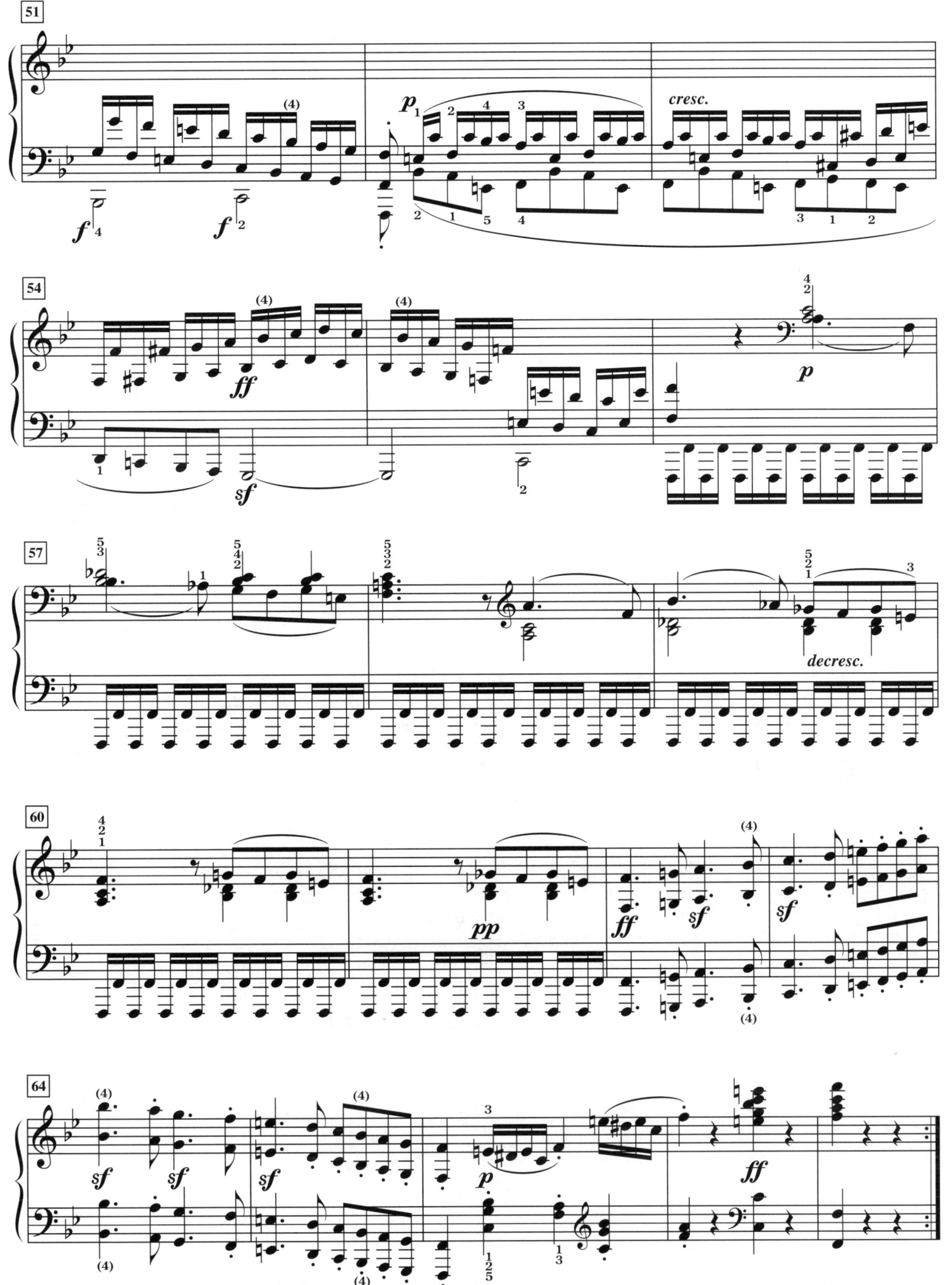

(f) The dynamic indication *p* appears in the first edition at the beginning of measure 101. Many editors have questioned the correctness of the marking because of the decrescendo in measure 104 followed by the dynamic indication of *p* in measure 105. D'Albert, Casella, Krebs, Martienssen, Schenker, and Schnabel simply delete the indication in measure 101. Köhler includes it without comment. Bülow, Geoffroy, Tovey, and Wallner acknowledge its existence, but question its correctness. Arrau includes it and suggests an editorial *ff* at the end of measure 103.

(g) Beats 1 and 3 are marked *rf* in the first edition, but all of the referenced editors change the markings to *sf* to correspond with those in measure 13.

159
f
sf
164
sf
decresc.
pp
170
175
cresc.
178
f

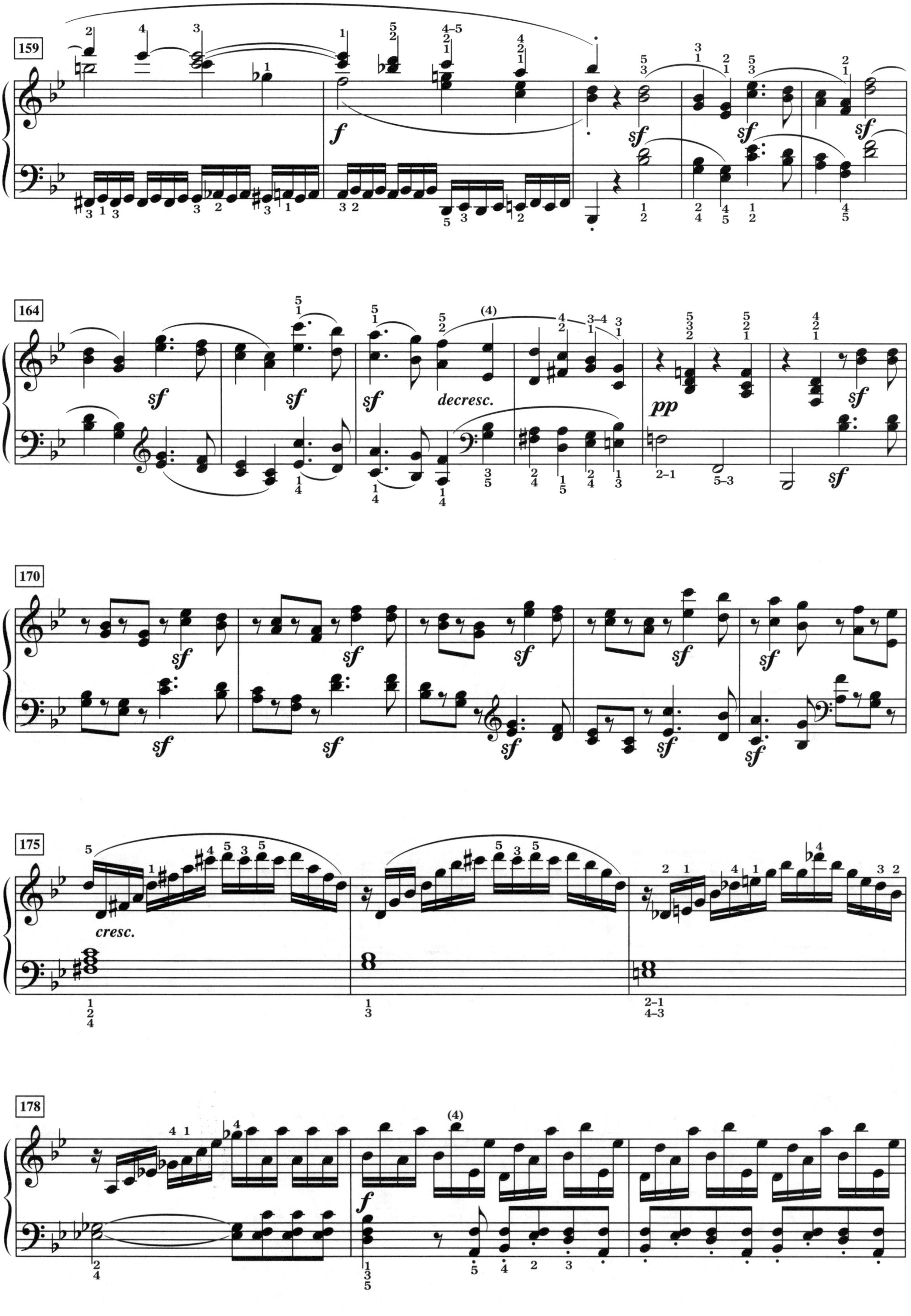

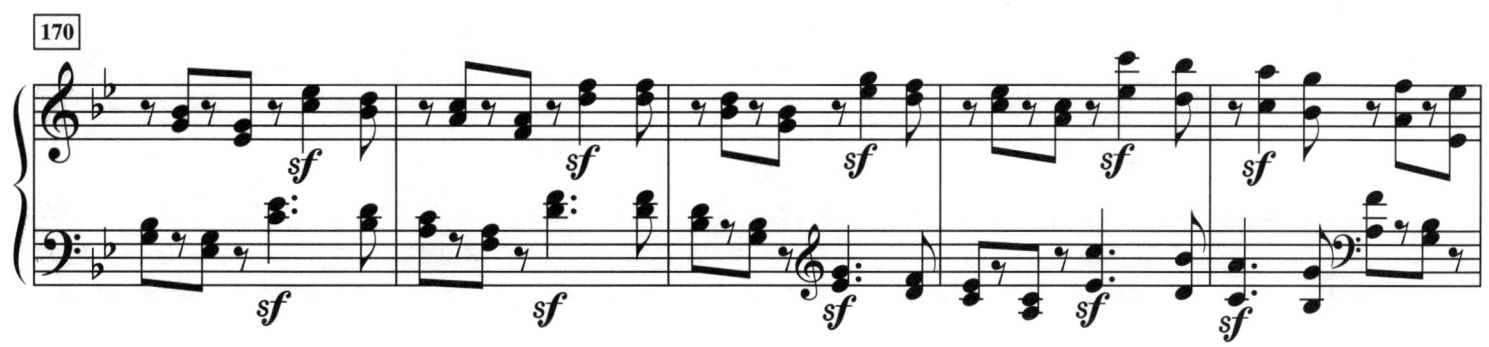

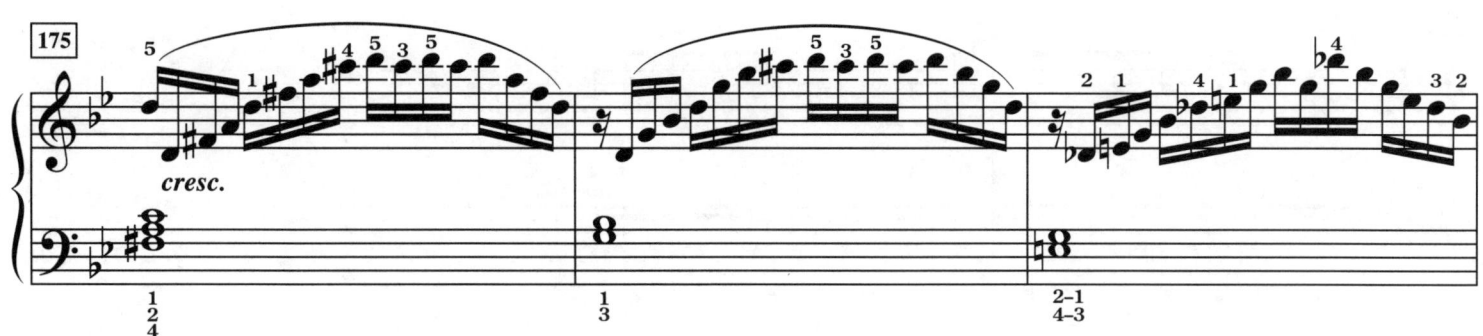

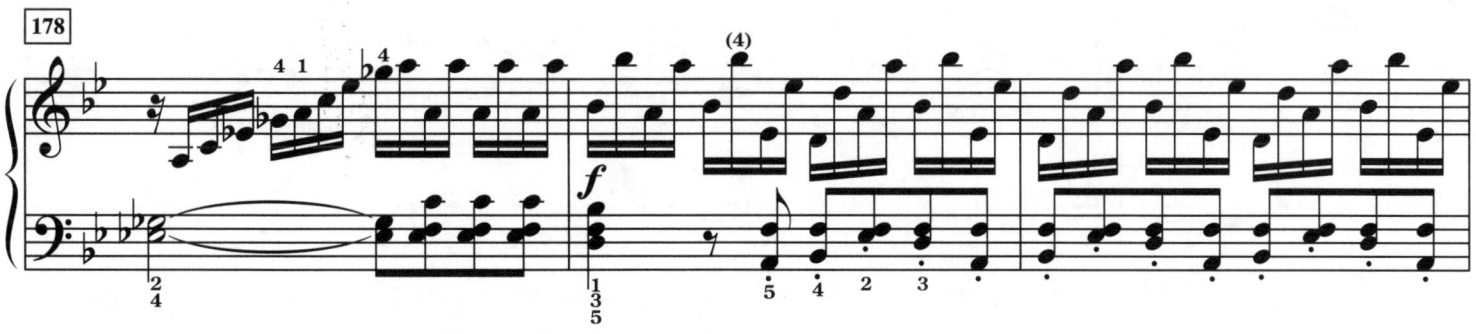

Adagio con molta espressione

ⓐ Although the first edition only occasionally marks the single grace notes in this movement with a slash through the stem (♪), this editor agrees with Schenker in calling for short appoggiaturas. On-the-beat execution conforms to period practice, albeit the difference between a rapid grace note before the beat and one on the beat is but scarcely audible.

ⓑ Several of the referenced editors offer realizations of the turn that appears in this measure and in measure 49.

Arrau, Schnabel, Tovey, and this editor:

Casella, Köhler, and Martienssen:

Bülow and Schenker like a quicker turn:

ⓒ Opinions of the referenced editors differ regarding the execution of the trills that occur in measures 8, 10, 13, 56, and 58.

Fingering that suggests starting on the upper note is offered by Arrau, Köhler, Tovey, and Wallner, and is preferred by this editor. Arrau's fingering spells out a six-note figure, preferable in this context to a simple four-note turn:

measure 8:

Finger indications of d'Albert, Bülow, Geoffroy, Martienssen, Schenker, and Schnabel suggest starting on the main note. Bülow realizes the ornament in a footnote, using a seven-note figure, quite possible at the slow tempo of the movement:

measure 8:

A five-note figure also works well.

Köhler apparently doesn't like the sound of the interval of a fourth that is produced by the double notes on beat 7 in measures 10, 13, 56, and 58, so he shifts in these spots to starting on the main note (except in measure 10, where he forgets to make the change.)

ⓓ In the first edition, the turn sign is placed clearly over the first sixteenth note on beat 2 of this measure and measure 67. However, all of the nine referenced editors who somehow address this ornament agree on playing the turn before beat 2, starting on the upper note:

measure 20:

Schnabel acknowledges the above execution but prefers:

measure 20:

(e) Only three of the referenced editors offer advice for this ornament and its counterpart in measure 77. According to C.P.E. Bach, the "three-toned slide" should be played on the beat, and very expressively in slow movements. Arrau and this editor prefer to follow C.P.E. Bach's direction:

measure 30:

Tovey agrees, but he suggests that the A-natural in the lower voice of the RH be delayed until after the slide, thus being played with the second C. Bülow's footnote insists the slide be played before the downbeat, robbing time from the final RH C of the preceding measure.

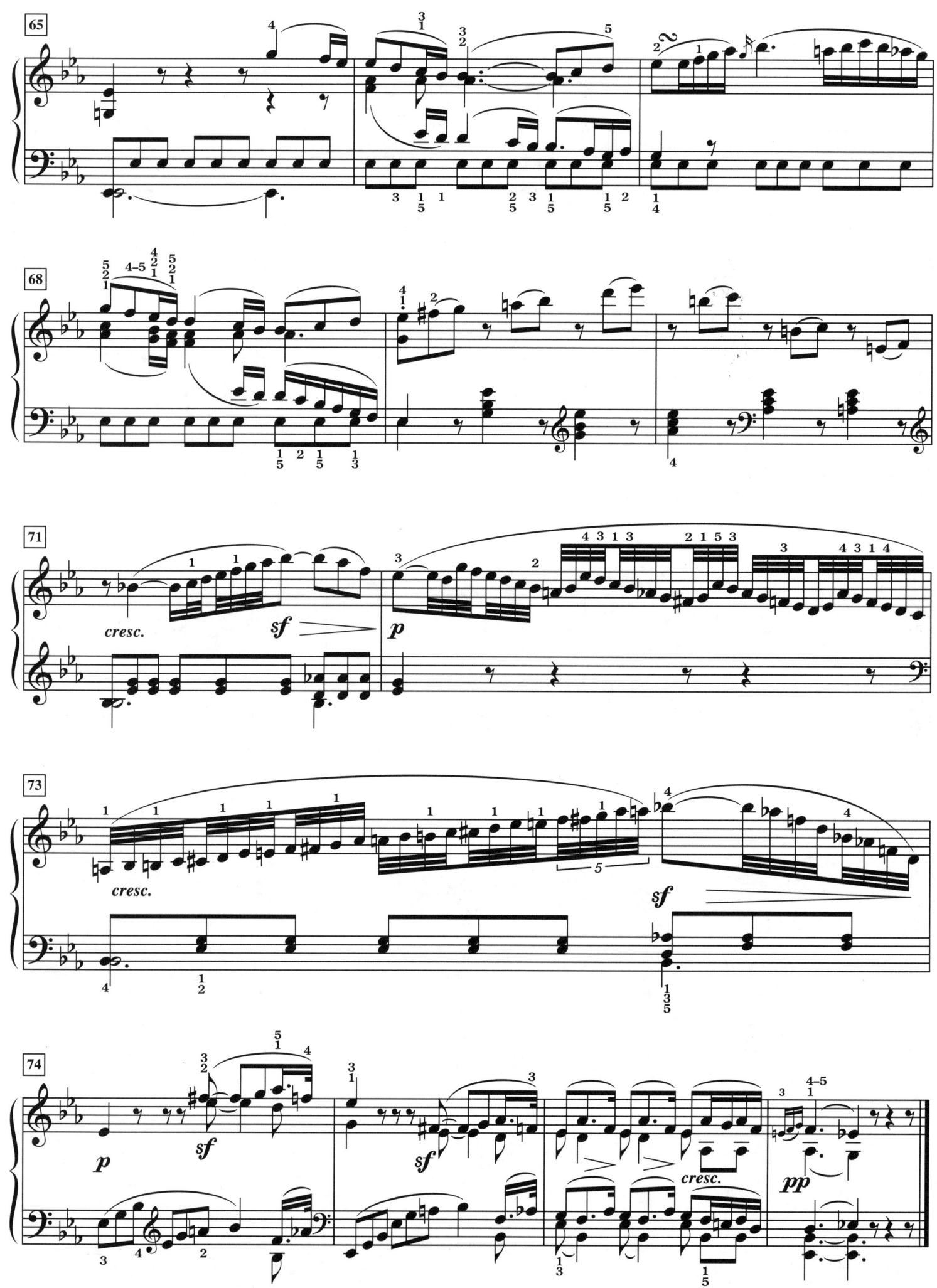

(a) Of the referenced editors only Arrau and Bülow offers advice on the grace notes that appear throughout this movement. They suggest rapid execution on the beat (played with the LH eighth note rather than before it). Such execution conforms to period practice. This editor agrees.

ⓒ The LH phrasing follows the first edition. Of the referenced editors, only d'Albert shows the first edition phrasing. The others alter the pattern to conform to that of measures 1, 17, and 24, some using a staccato on the first eighth note of measure 26, others not adding it. In the opinion of this editor, the first edition phrasing is validated by the phrasing in the alto voice, its presence preventing the other measures from being exactly analogous.

ⓓ Beethoven provided no dynamic markings for the Minore section. Eleven of the referenced editors offer their suggestions, eight opting for *f* and three for *mf*.

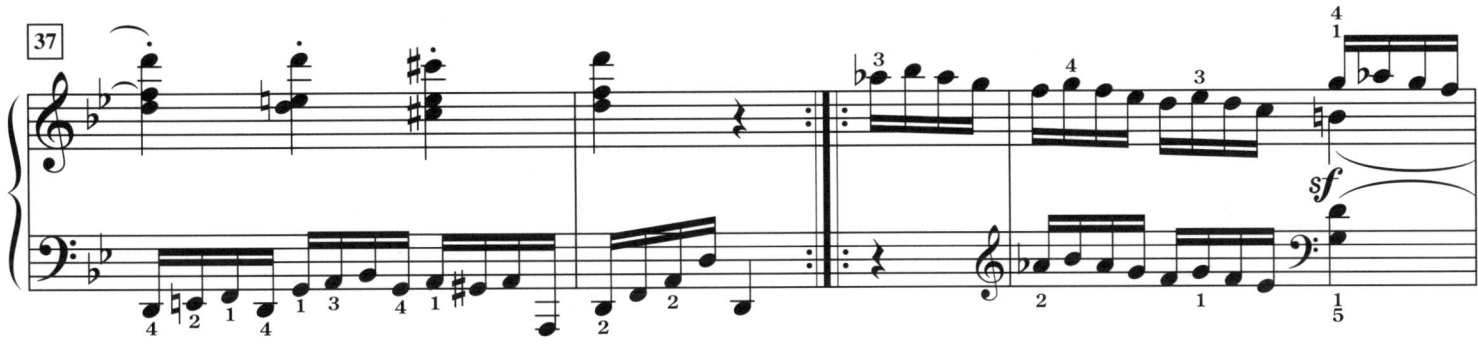

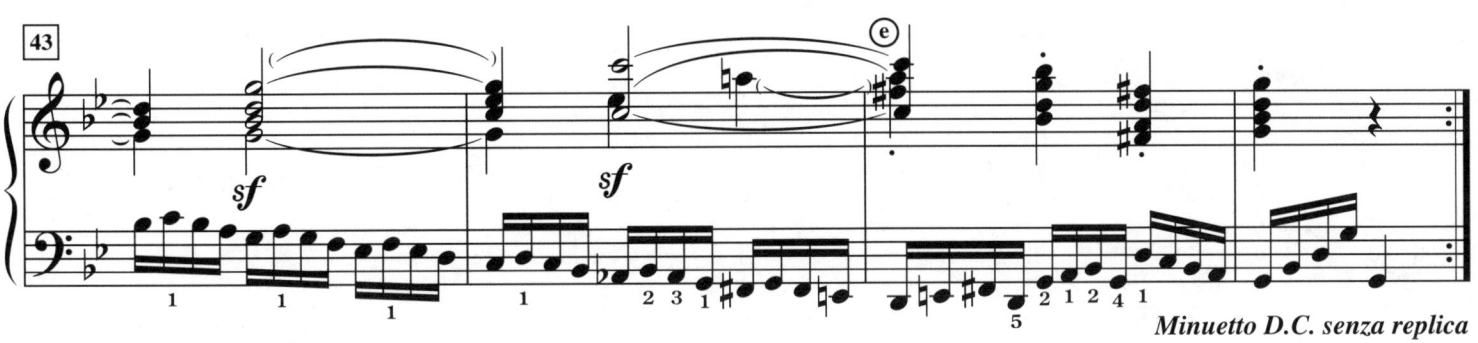

Minuetto D.C. senza replica

(e) The RH A-naturals at the end of measures 44 and the downbeat of measure 45 are not tied in the first edition. Six of the referenced editors, Arrau, Bülow, Köhler, Martienssen, Schenker, and Tovey, assume the tie is missing and add it, a decision with which this editor agrees. Casella simply leaves the A-natural out of the chord on the downbeat of measure 45.

RONDO

Allegretto

ⓐ The first edition shows the RH slur of measure 1 concluding at the end of the measure, followed by a two-note slur on the first two eighth notes of measure 2. Similar slurring occurs at measures 3–4 and 7–8. When the opening theme is stated in measures 49–57, as well as measures 152–156, this articulation is no longer used, but rather RH slurs join the upbeats of the earlier measures with the first two eighth notes of the next measures. This variation is noted in this edition as possibly intended, a point of view consistent with the fact that the composer varies this theme each time it appears. All of the referenced editors disregard this difference to some extent. Casella, Köhler, Schnabel, and Tovey apply the longer slur patterns to measures 1–8. D'Albert, Arrau, Bülow, Geoffroy, Krebs, Martienssen, Schenker, and Wallner all adopt an inexplicable arrangement, showing long slurs at measures 1–2 and 3–4, but leaving intact the break between measures 7 and 8.

ⓑ Fingering of the referenced editors suggests that they all start this trill (measures 17, 66, 128, and 181) on the main note except Arrau, who characteristically prefers the older tradition and begins on the upper note. Starting on the main note, one can choose a five-note figure, perhaps somewhat simplistic, but easy to play:

or a seven-note figure, harder and a bit treacherous:

Although unusual, Arrau's realization does conform to tradition, resulting in a six-note pattern that seems both sufficient and comfortable to this editor:

[Musical notation: measures 18-30]

ⓒ As with the preceding ornament, all the referenced editors who offer fingering start the ornament in measures 19 and 130 on the main note, except Arrau, who starts on the upper note. With one exception, these editors do not write out the ornament, but one might assume the following realization:

The exception is Schenker who, in a partial realization, suggests a different rhythmic figure:

Arrau's realization uses Schenker's rhythmic pattern starting on the upper note:

ⓓ The first edition places the turn signs over the dotted sixteenth notes that occur on the second half of beats 1 and 2 in measures 21, 132, and 134. All of the referenced editors except Arrau recommend playing the turn before these sixteenth notes:

Schnabel acknowledges the preceding pattern, but states his preference for another realization before the dotted sixteenth note:

D'Albert, Bülow, Casella, Köhler, Krebs, Martienssen, and Schnabel actually move the turn signs to the left in these measures so that they visually support the above realizations. Arrau, Geoffroy, Schenker, Tovey, and Wallner reproduce the turn signs as they appear in the first edition. Wallner does not address these realizations. Geoffroy, Schnabel, and Tovey subscribe to the realizations before the dotted sixteenth.

Arrau suggests a more literal interpretation of the text:

It is interesting to note that Arrau does not apply such a literal approach to measures 20 and 67 of the second movement of this work, where he moves the ornaments to the left, apparently to accommodate the more usual realization.

(e) As in earlier footnotes, all the referenced editors except Arrau start the ornaments in measures 42 and 43 on the main note. All recommend adding closing notes (*nachschlag*):

measure 42:

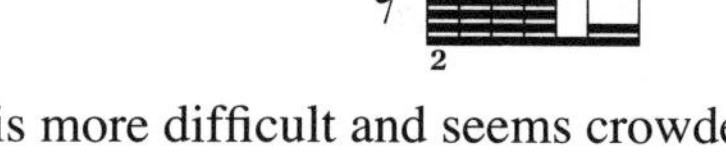

Arrau's starting on the upper note results in a six-note ornament, one that is more difficult and seems crowded in this context. Whatever realization is decided upon can be applied to measure 154.

ⓕ The first edition shows no tie between the two E's that are written as the last LH eighth note of measures 138 and the first eighth note of measure 139. Nine of the referenced editors deem the tie missing and provide it without comment. D'Albert, Krebs, and Schnabel show no tie. Schnabel obviously believes the first edition is correct, for he provides fingering for two LH notes on the downbeat of measure 139.

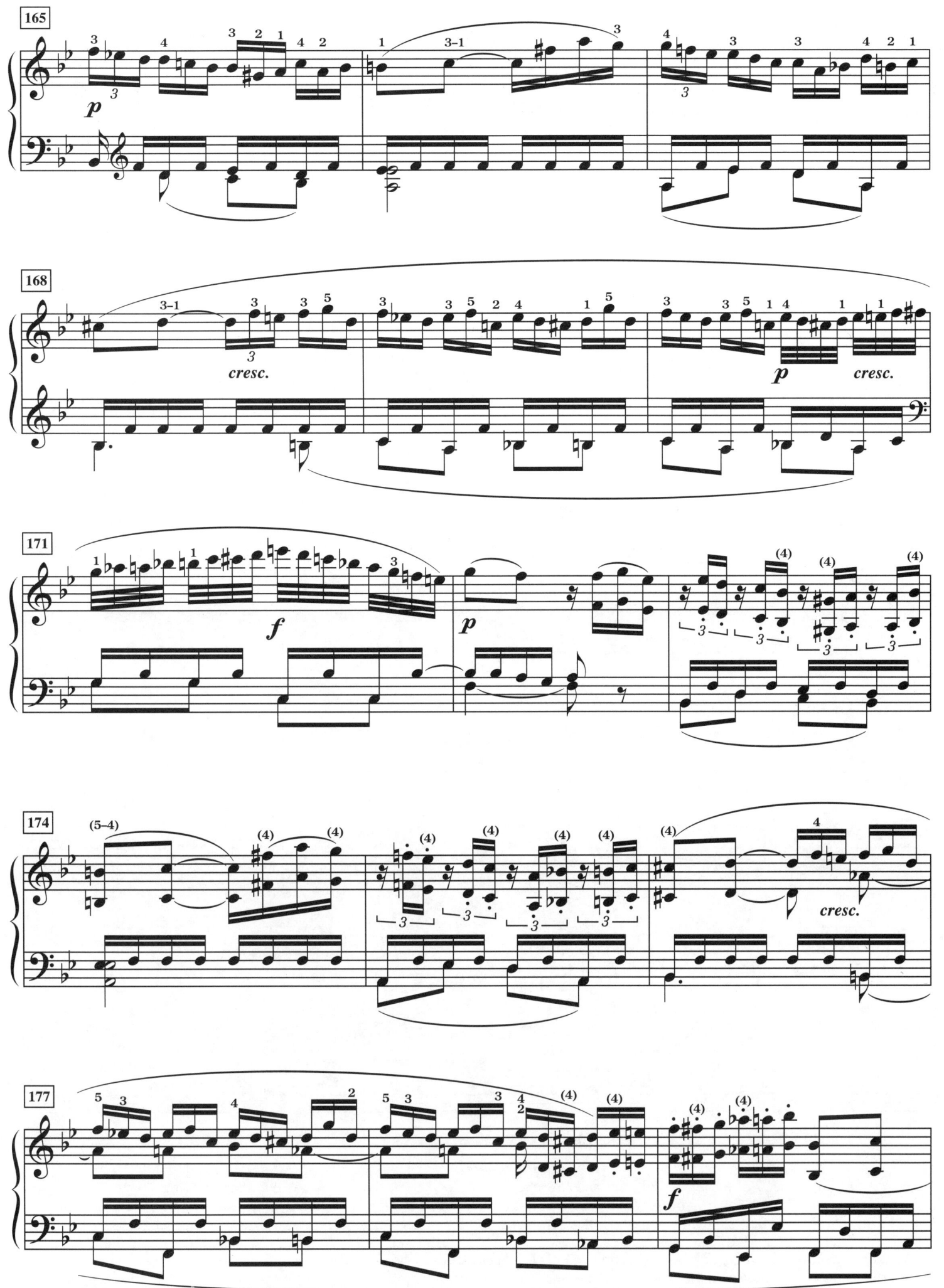

(g) On the RH downbeats of measures 189, 191, and 193, the first edition shows staccato marks over the top B-flats in addition to the ends of ties from the quarter notes of the preceding measures. This seeming contradiction has resulted in different opinions as to whether the B-flats should be played on the downbeats. Judging from suggested fingering of the referenced editors, six of them (Arrau, Köhler, Martienssen, Schenker, Schnabel, and Wallner), as well as this editor, honor the tie, reasoning that the staccato applies only to the inner voices: Three editors (d'Albert, Bülow, and Geoffroy) honor the staccato and would have the performer play the B-flats on the downbeats. The remaining three editors offer neither advice nor fingering that reveals their preference in this matter.

About Op. 26

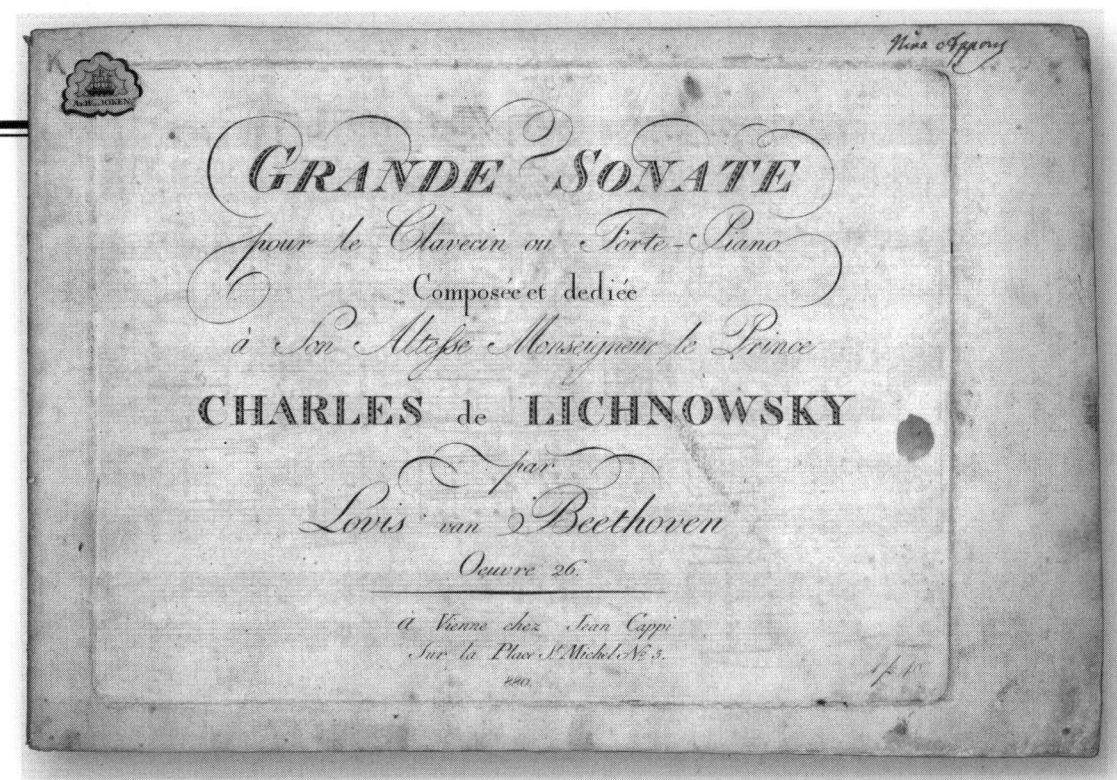

Op. 26 title page from the first edition, reproduced by kind permission from the copy in the Austrian National Library, Hoboken Collection, S. H. Beethoven 125

The sonata, Op. 26, is distinctive for several reasons. In the first place, this sonata is the first of a small group, each of which is experimental. Thus, the Op. 26 and the two sonatas that comprise the Op. 27 are works in which the composer sets aside the classical models that characterize his piano sonatas up to this point. In the case of the Op. 26, a theme and five variations replace the expected sonata-allegro first movement, a substitution that Mozart had already used in his Sonata in A Major, K. 331, for piano. In addition, the order of the slow movement and the dance movement in the four-movement structure is reversed, so that the scherzo appears second in the work, and the slow movement third. This switch is significant, one that several later composers adopt in their sonatas—Frédéric Chopin (1810–1849), Alexander Scriabin (1872–1915), Sergei Prokofiev (1891–1953), and Samuel Barber (1910–1981), for example. The third movement is a funeral march "on the death of a hero," and thus somewhat programmatic. Finally, the Op. 26 is the first sonata of Beethoven for which the autograph is extant. (Fragmented sketches also exist in sketchbooks from the summer of 1801, as well as in a notebook dating 1800.)[33]

The Op. 26 was announced for publication in the *Wiener Zeitung* on March 3, 1802, by Giovanni Cappi (1765–1815). Cappi had been employed by Artaria. He became a partner in the firm in 1792, four years before Artaria published Beethoven's Op. 2 sonatas. Cappi left Artaria around 1800 to establish his own firm. It stands to reason that he would seek out Beethoven for new works and, indeed, he published both the Op. 26 and the Op. 27 set of piano sonatas.

Like the Sonata No. 8 in C Minor, Op. 13, the Sonata No. 12 in A-flat Major, Op. 26, is dedicated to Prince Karl von Lichnowsky (1761–1814). Beethoven lived in the Lichnowsky household for several years after he came to Vienna, and the Prince and his wife, Maria Christiane (1765–1841), not only supported Beethoven financially, but also hosted gatherings in their home at which many of the composer's works were played for the first time. Beethoven sometimes resented this assistance and occasionally complained about being oppressed by what he perceived as demands by the Lichnowskys. On balance, however, the composer valued the couple's support and friendship, and the Prince remained steadfastly loyal to Beethoven through the years. In about 1800, Lichnowsky granted Beethoven a stipend of 600 gulden a year (a little over $2,000) so that the composer might feel more independent financially. This stipend remained in place at least until 1805.

---

[33] Karl Lothar Mikulicz, *Ein Notierungsbuch von Beethoven (1800)* (Leipzig: Breitkopf & Härtel, 1927), indexed on p. 28.

Sonata No. 12 in A-flat Major (Grande Sonate), Op. 26

Autograph/facsimile:	survived
Sketches/loose pages:	yes
First edition:	Cappi: Vienna, 1802

The first movement of the Op. 26, marked *Andante con Variazioni*, with its lyrical opening theme seems to have suggested extra-musical elaboration. Beethoven himself sought a text for it at one point. Moreover, an Austrian music critic who befriended Beethoven, Johann Friedrich Rochlitz (1769–1842), wrote a 28-page descriptive program for these variations. This embellishment appeared in his four-volume work entitled *Für Freunde der Tonkunst*, published sometime between 1824 and 1832, and centered around the private life of an elderly law clerk! Beethoven's student Carl Czerny described the opening theme as "noble," with an "almost religious character." Czerny then proceeds to assign a different character with different metronome markings to each of the following variations.[34] (See page 90).

The structure of the first movement is quite formal. The theme itself has a small **A A B A** format. Each of the five variations follows this pattern. The third variation is in the parallel minor, and the composer uses the formidable-looking key signature for A-flat minor of seven flats. The final variation introduces a written-out trill, an early indication of a device that the composer will use more extensively in the variations that occur in both the Sonatas No. 30 in E Major, Op. 109, and No. 32 in C Minor, Op. 111. A short coda follows the fifth variation and closes out the movement.

The *Allegro molto* scherzo follows the expected minuet and trio plan with the exception of the opening **A** section, which is marked not to be repeated (*La primi parte senza repetizione*), possibly because the 16-measure section itself repeats the first eight measures. The movement is in the tonic key of the sonata with a trio in the subdominant, D-flat major.

Beethoven indicates that the third movement is a funeral march on the death of a hero (*Marcia funebre sulla morte d'un Eroe*). The person so honored is not identified, but Beethoven was one of several composers of the period who were attracted by the idea of writing music that was involved with the concept of heroic death, an interest that is thought to be a spin-off from the French Revolution. Thus, in 1797 Luigi Cherubini (1760–1842) wrote a *Hymn and Funeral March on the Death of General Hoche*, and similar examples can be noted in the music of François-Joseph Gossec (1734–1829) and Etienne-Nicolas Méhul (1763–1817). Two friends of Beethoven, Franz Gerhard Wegeler (1765–1848) and Ferdinand Ries (1784–1838), claimed that Beethoven was influenced by an opera popular at the time.[35] Ferdinando Paer's (1771–1839) *Achille* did, indeed, contain a funeral march in C Minor, but its influence can be questioned, for the opera was not produced until 1801, postdating sketches of the march in the Op. 26. Beethoven's interest in heroic death does appear in several works other than the Op. 26: *Cantata on the Death of Emperor Joseph II* (1790); the Symphony No. 3 ("Eroica"), Op. 55 (1803–04); *Christ on the Mount of Olives*, Op. 85 (1803–04); and the incidental music to Goeth's *Egmont*, Op. 84 (1809–10).

---

[34] Carl Czerny, *On the Proper Performance of All Beethoven's Works for the Piano*, ed. Paul Badura-Skoda (Vienna: Universal Edition, 1970), p. 37.

[35] Franz Gerhard Wegeler and Ferdinand Ries, *Biographische Notizen über Beethoven* (Koblenz: K. Bädeker, 1838), p. 48.

The use of the tremolo figures (measures 31, 32, 35 and 36) in the trio of the third movement by Beethoven is thought possibly to have been influenced by the composer-pianist Daniel Steibelt (1765–1823). Steibelt deserted the Prussian army as a youth, fled to Paris, where he established a career as a pianist, composer, and pedagogue. After a dispute with his publisher, Steibelt went to London, where his opera *Albert and Adelaide* was produced at Covent Garden. He traveled back to Germany in 1799 and by 1800 turned up in Vienna where Count Moritz von Fries (1777–1826) arranged a competition in his home between Beethoven and Steibelt. (Such events were frequently staged by those who supported musicians in order to show off the artists in whom they had invested.) It was reported that although Beethoven won the bout, Steibelt truly amazed his audience with the effect of his tremolos. In fact, years later Charles-Louis Hanon (1819–1900) reported in his most famous set of exercises that Steibelt "used to make his audience shiver by his tremolo."[36] Beethoven's use of the devise in the Op. 26 is also effective but, indeed, quite discreet.

In 1815, Beethoven undertook to provide incidental music for a drama by Friedrich Duncker (d. 1842) entitled *Leonore Probaska* (WoO 96). Duncker was a cabinet member to the King of Prussia and was in Vienna officially for the Congress of 1814. For Duncker's dramatic project Beethoven wrote new material in the form of a *Romanze* and a *Melodram*. In addition, he orchestrated the funeral march from Op. 26, transposed to B minor. Although a production of the theater piece never materialized, the orchestral version of the funeral march was played years later at the composer's own funeral, held on March 29, 1827.

The formal pattern of the third movement is one that is associated with march music, **A B A**, where the **B** section is a trio in two parts, each marked to be repeated. The outer sections are in A-flat minor with the aforementioned key signature, the trio section in A-flat major. The outer sections present an internal pattern of **A A B A** (**A** = measures 1–8; **A** = upbeat to 9–16; **B** = upbeat to 17–20; **A** = upbeat to 21–30), the second statement of **A** starting in B minor and modulating to D major. The movement closes with a heart-rending eight-measure coda.

Czerny claims that the final movement of the Op. 26 was influenced by the work of Johann Baptist Cramer (1771–1858). Cramer had been born in Germany, but early in his career moved to London, where he studied with Muzio Clementi (1752–1832). In September of 1799 Cramer visited Vienna for several months. During this period he met and befriended Beethoven.

According to Czerny, while in Veinna Cramer created a "great sensation" with his "three sonatas" (Op. 23), dedicated to Jospeh Haydn and published by Artaria. Czerny cites the first of these, also in A-flat major, as being influential on Beethoven's concept of this movement.[37]

The rondo pattern is regular in the *Allegro* final movement: **A B A C A B** (**A** = measures 1–28; transition = 28–32; **B** = 32–52; **A** = 52–80; **C** = 80–99; **A** = 99–130; transition = 130–138; **B** = 138–154) with a short coda based on figuration generated from **A** (measures 154–169). The **C** section is in two parts, but only the first of the two, in C minor, is marked to be repeated, the second part acting as a transition back to **A**. The movement is compact, presenting non-stop sixteenth notes almost without interruption. Following a funeral march with a perpetual motion movement is a combination that Chopin is to use approximately four decades later in his Op. 35 sonata, although the mood of Beethoven's final movement is more cheerful than that of Chopin.

---

[36] Charles-Louis Hanon, *Der Clavier-Virtuose* (Leipzig: Otto Junne, n.d.), p. 110.
[37] Czerny, Op. cit., p. 38.

Dedicated to the Prince Karl von Lichnowsky

Sonata No. 12 in A-flat Major
(Grande Sonate)

Ludwig van Beethoven (1770–1827)
Op. 26

ⓐ Bülow and Casella add arpeggiation to the chord on the downbeat of measure 4, Bülow justifying the addition in a footnote by citing other examples in the sonatas where Beethoven uses arpeggiation. D'Albert cautions against playing it as a broken chord in a footnote. The remaining editors of the referenced group let the chord stand as it appears in both the autograph and the first edition. Playing the chord solidly, however, may be impossible for small hands. In such cases this editor recommends the following compromise in preference to arpeggiation, using the pedal to capture the sonority of the tied bass note. This arrangement preserves the effect of the dissonance:

ⓑ The autograph of this sonata shows all grace notes of this figure (measures 4, 12, 15, 30, 33, 38, 46, 64, 72, 80, 98, 174, 182, and 200) as eighth notes without slashes across the stems. Moreover, the small eighth notes are set apart distinctly from the following four thirty-second notes, often by a rather wide space. Such a presentation suggests to this editor executing the grace notes before the beat with as much melodic import as time allows. None of the referenced editors address whether the grace notes should come before the beat or on the beat. Schenker leaves the original notation but calls for short appoggiaturas in a footnote. Arrau, Geoffroy, Krebs, Schnabel, and Wallner preserve the original notation. D'Albert, Bülow, Casella, Köhler, Martienssen, and Tovey alter the grace notes by placing slashes through the stems.

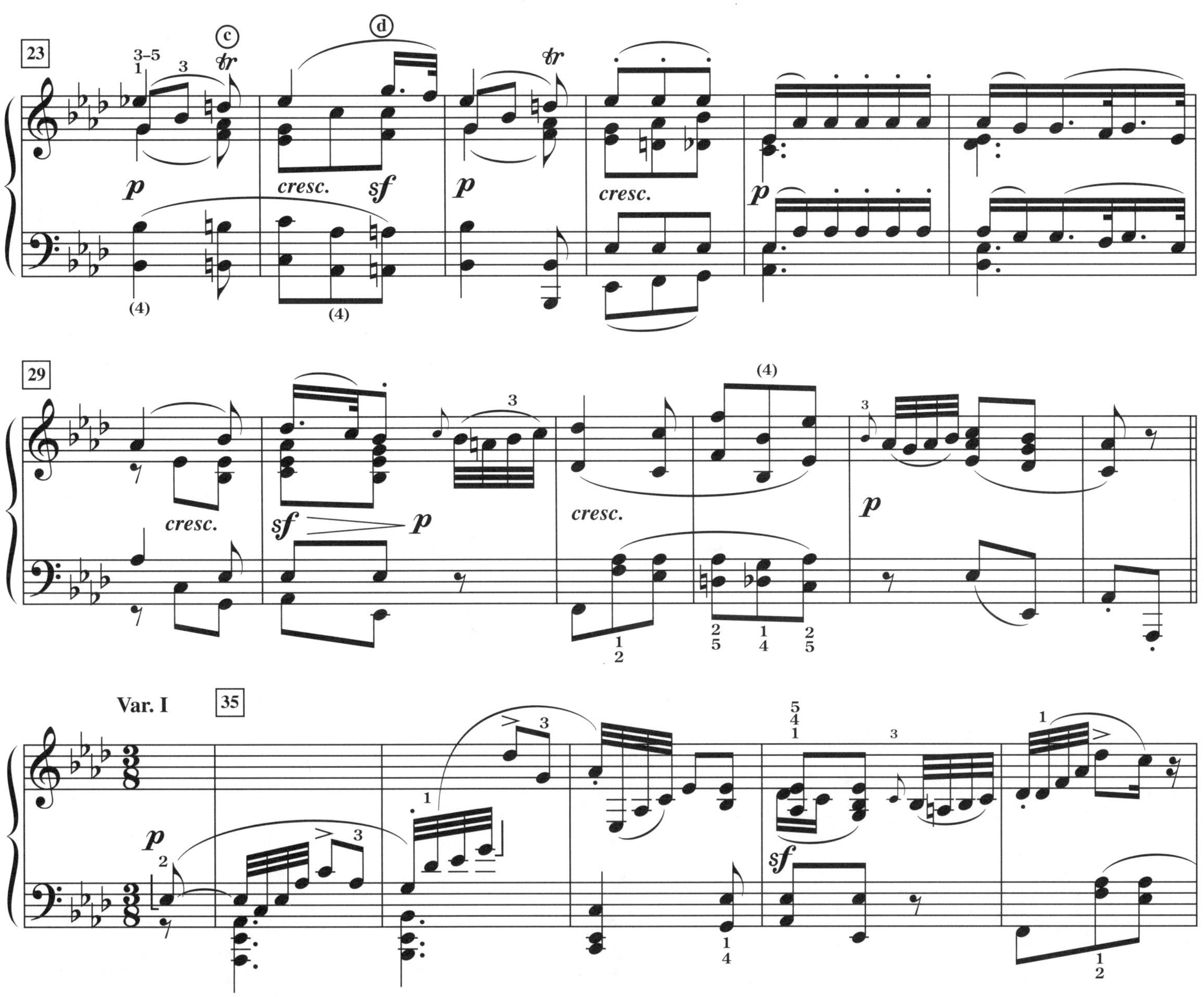

ⓒ Of the referenced editors who offer suggestions for the trill in measures 23, 25, and 59, all add closing notes (*nachschlagen*), although none are in the first edition or measures 23 and 59 of the autograph. Small marks in measure 25 of the autograph might be read as ending notes, but it is difficult to be sure. Certainly, the musicality of the phrase suggests them; thus the tradition for them is strong. Nine editors start the trill on the main note, several suggesting the following rhythms:

measure 23: or autograph measure 25:

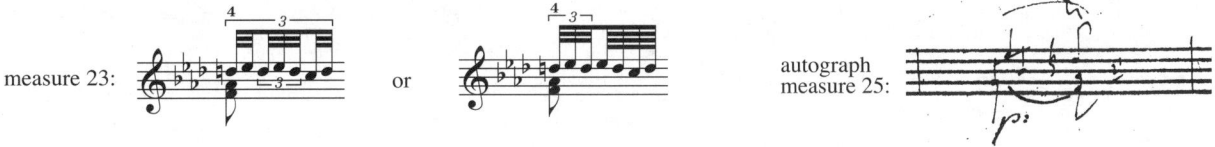

This editor prefers the first of the above realizations. Arrau alone recommends starting on the upper note, using a six-note pattern that includes closing notes.

ⓓ Performers whose hands are unable to reach the RH intervals of a ninth in measures 24 and 26 will have to arpeggiate. This editor recommends playing the lowermost note of the arpeggio with the RH thumb, on the beat, pedaling each eighth note. The pedal depressions in measure 26 need to be short enough to preserve the *portato* indication.

ⓔ The LH slurs indicated in measure 90 and 92 represent this editor's reading of the autograph. Measure 92 of the autograph clearly presents a three-note slur. The slur in measure 90, however, is less clear, for it begins between the last sixteenth and the two thirty-seconds. It should also be noted that the composer discontinued writing staccato marks for the LH sixteenth notes at measure 88 with the expectation that the performer will understand that they should continue. He reestablishes the staccato touch by placing marks over the first four LH sixteenth notes of measure 91 and the six LH sixteenth notes of measure 93. One might assume that he did this to prompt the performer to return to the staccato touch in each case after the preceding slurred phrases. This first edition differs from the autograph, for it shows only the two thirty-second notes slurred in measure 90, but a three-note slur in measure 92. Of the referenced editors, nine show slurs only over the two thirty-second notes in both measures 90 and 92. Geoffroy and Wallner acknowledge the way the early sources present measure 92 in footnotes, but print two note slurs in the main body of the score. Arrau follows the first edition by presenting a two-note slur in measure 90 and a three-note slur in measure 92. This editor believes both measure 90 and 92 contain three-note slurs.

(f) The autograph shows staccato marks on the beat 2 of measures 137, 138, 139, 140, and 141, but the first edition does not show these staccato marks. Of the referenced editors, nine follow the first edition. This editor joins Martienssen, Schenker, and Tovey in following the autograph. Staccato marks do not appear in conjunction with this two-note figure in any other measures of this variation, either in the autograph or the first edition.

(g) For the first time in the sonatas, Beethoven indicates the use of the damper pedal by writing the term *senza sordino*, meaning "without dampers" in this context. The use of the damper pedal with the crescendo in measure 216 results in a rich, colorful ending to this movement.

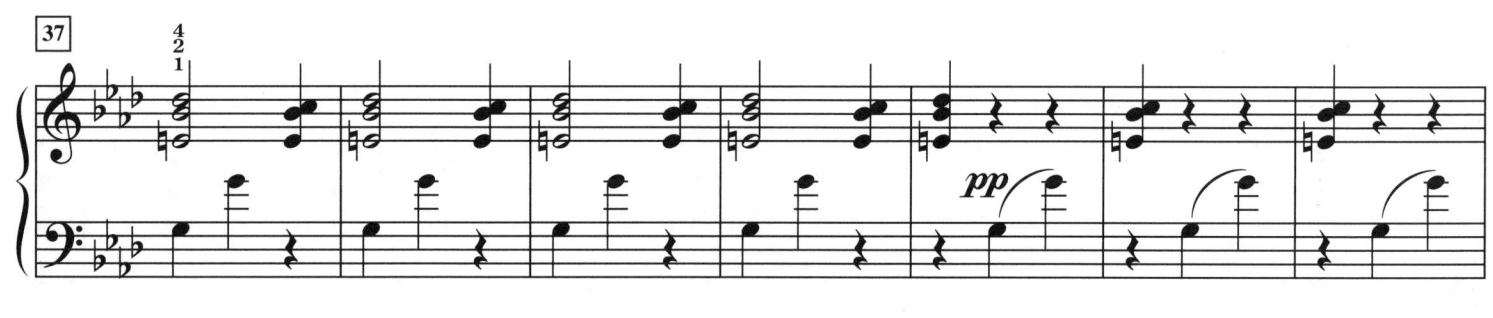

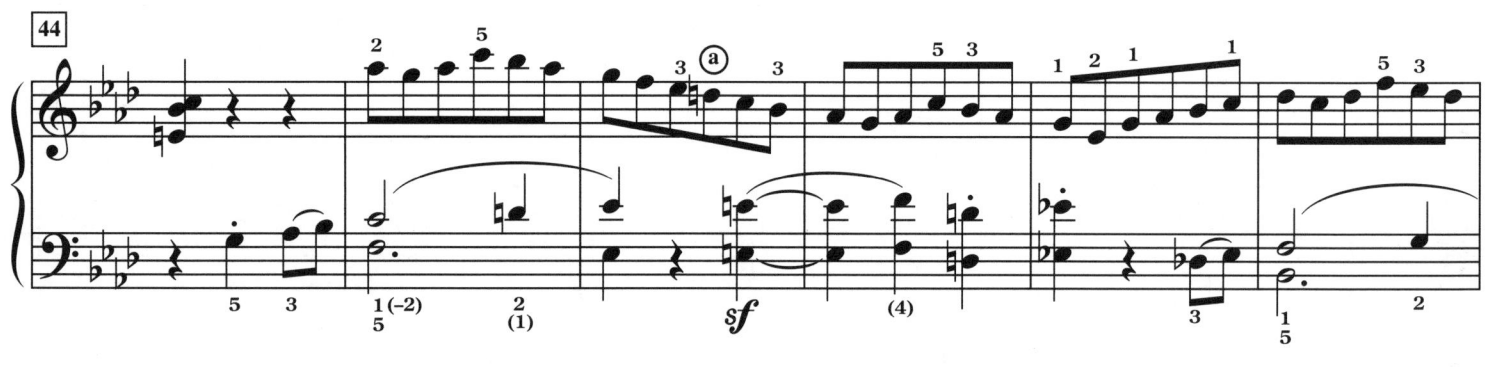

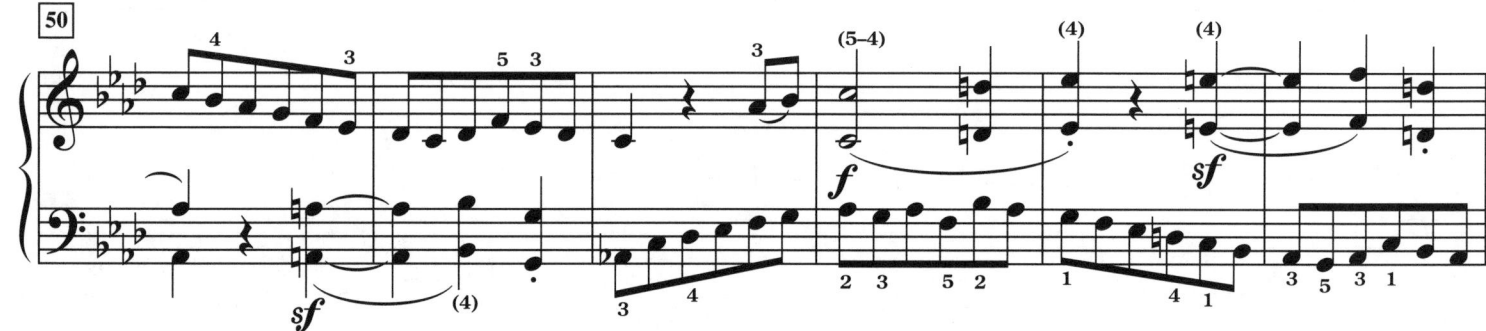

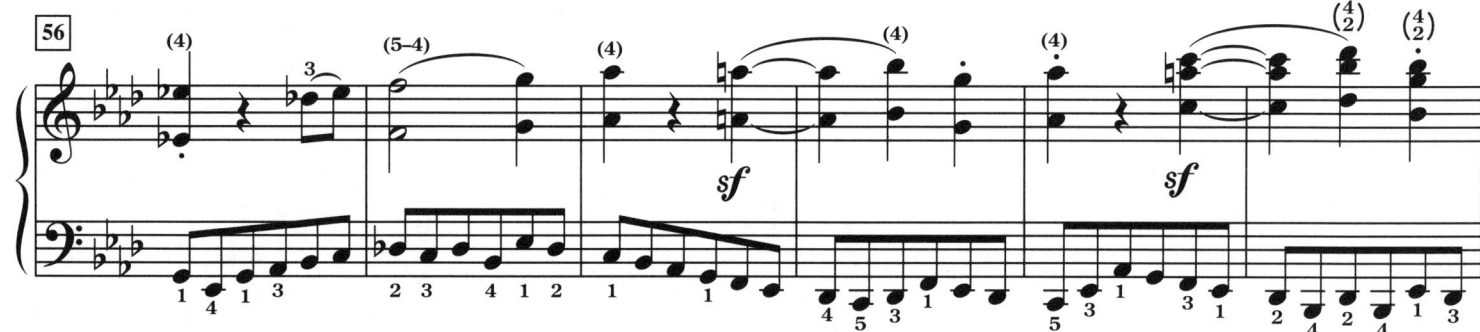

ⓐ The autograph shows D-flat in measure 46 in the RH and in measure 54 in the LH. The first edition shows D-natural in both places. Eight of the referenced editors use D-natural without comment. Geoffroy and Wallner use D-natural in the main body of the text but acknowledge the discrepancy in a footnote. Martienssen uses D-flat without comment. Schenker uses D-flat, acknowledges the discrepancy, and argues the D-flat suggests the overall A-flat tonality of the passage.

ⓑ Two discrepancies between the autograph and the first edition occur in measures 88–90. The autograph shows G-flat in the LH of measure 88. The first edition shows G-natural. All twelve editors prefer the G-natural and this editor agrees. A second discrepancy between the autograph and the first edition is that the autograph ends the RH slur at beat 2 of measure 90. The first edition prolongs the slur to the downbeat of measure 91. Seven of the referenced editors follow the first edition, using the longer slur. Bülow, Geoffroy, Martienssen, Schenker, and this editor prefer following the autograph. Wallner prints the longer slur in the 1952 edition, but changes it in the 1980 edition.

ⓐ Players with small hands may have to divide this chord, taking the low E-flat with the LH. In such a case, the lowermost A-flat should be sustained by catching it in the new sonority instituted by a pedal change on beat 4 of the measure.

ⓑ Both the autograph and the first edition place the *p* mark on beat 1 of measure 6. However, both place it on beat 4 in measure 45. Seven of the referenced editors change measure 6 to conform to measure 45 without comment. Geoffroy, Tovey, and Wallner follow the early sources, Geoffroy and Wallner footnoting the difference. Arrau and Casella not only note the difference but support markedly different renditions, Arrau by adding editorial dynamics in brackets and Casella in a footnote.

ⓒ At the beginning of measure 10, both the first edition and the autograph show the mark *f*. In measure 49, the first edition shows *sf*, thereby creating a slightly different effect. The autograph is ambiguous in measure 49, the *f* showing clearly, but the *s* preceding it, if it existed, is obscured by one of the notes of the chord. This ambiguity has led to a variety of renderings in editions. Eight of the referenced editors place *sf* markings on both measures 10 and 49 without comment. Schenker places *f* markings in both measures, thus following the autograph and reading measure 49 as showing only *f*. This editor agrees with Schenker. Arrau, Geoffroy, and Wallner follow the first edition, placing *f* at measure 10 and *sf* at measure 49. Arrau suggests by an editorial dynamic in brackets that both places should be marked *f*. Geoffroy suggests in a footnote that both places should be marked *sf*.

(d) Seven of the referenced editors indicate fingering that suggests starting this trill on the main note. This editor agrees. Only Arrau's fingering indicates starting on the upper auxiliary. Bülow offers a helpful realization of the trill:

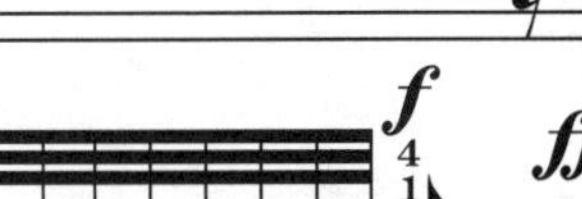

(e) Pedaling in measures 31, 32, 35, and 36 is indicated in both the autograph and the first edition by the terms *senza sordino* and *con sordino*, the first term being notated at the beginning of each tremolo and the second at the sixteenth note leading to the eighth note on beat 4. Eleven of the referenced editors, using contemporary pedaling indications (𝄢. ✻), have indicated a pedal release either on or just after the eighth note on beat 3. This editor agrees. Schenker, however, interprets the early indications differently and marks the pedal release at the sixteenth note before beat 4.

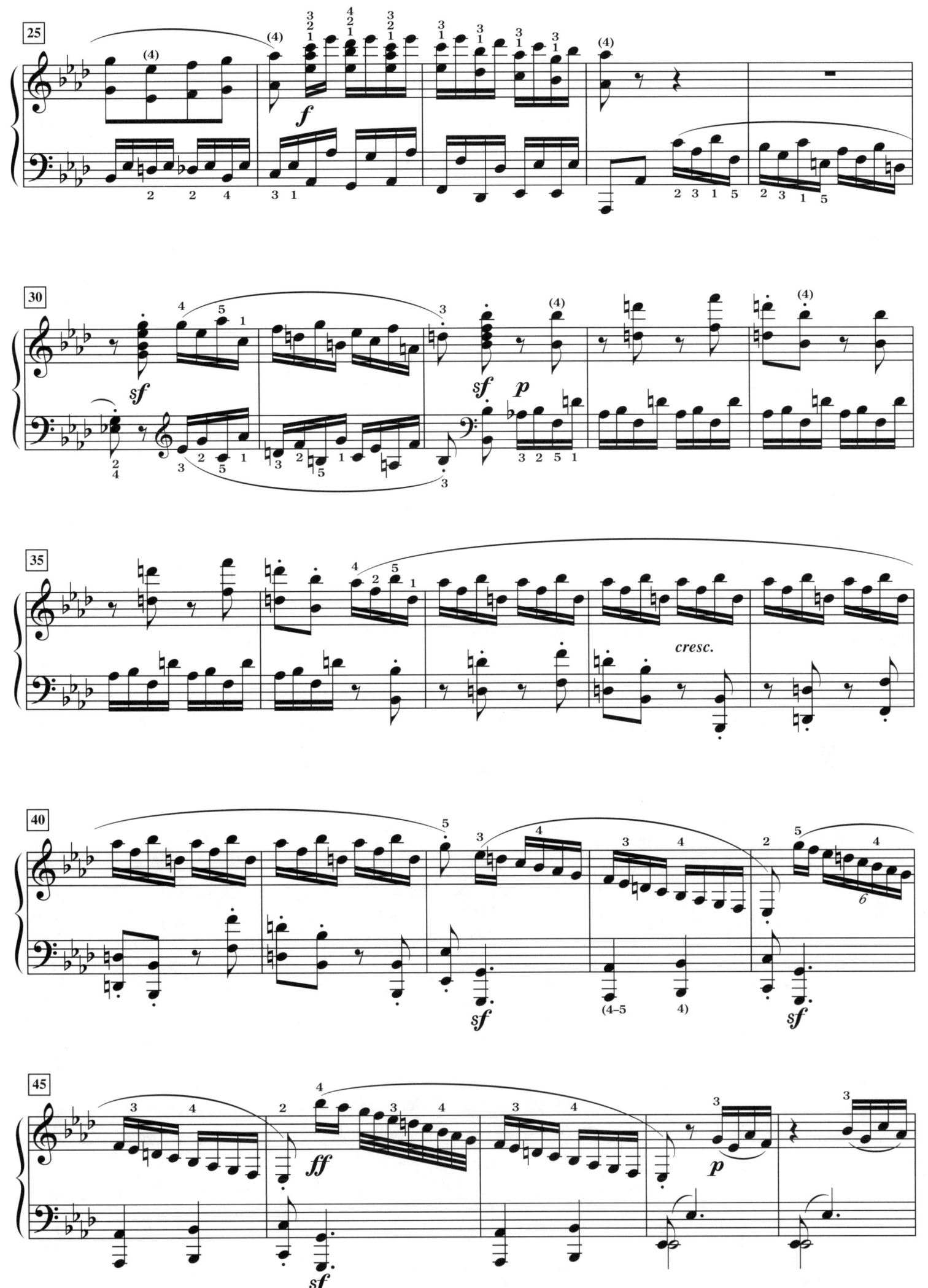

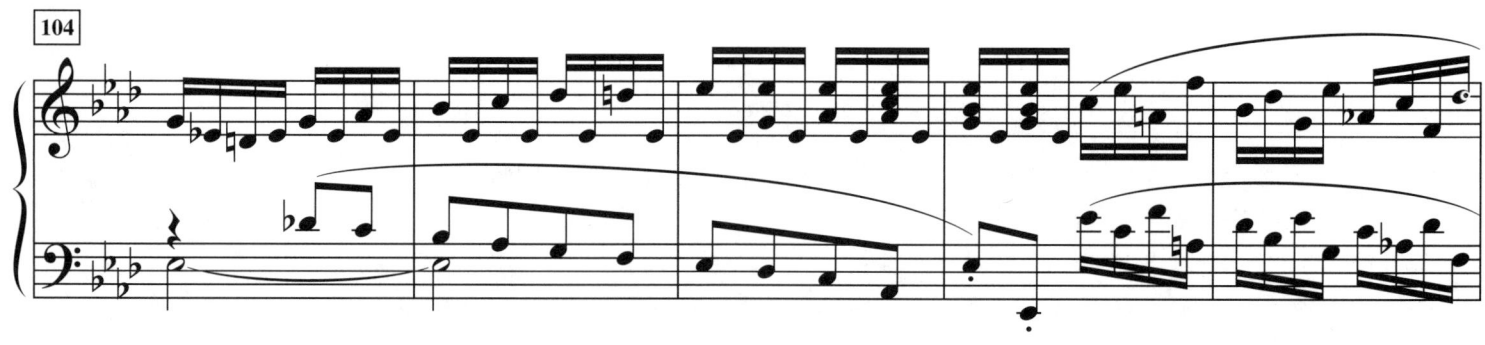
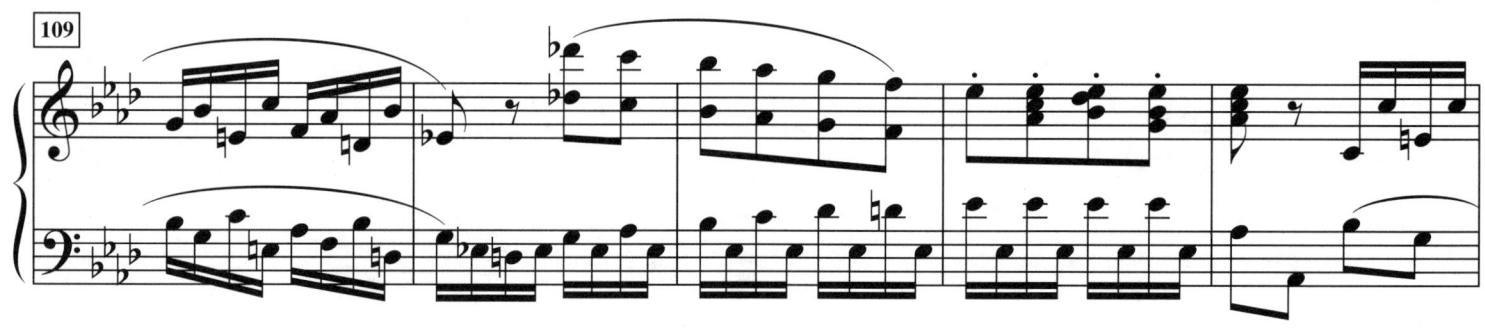

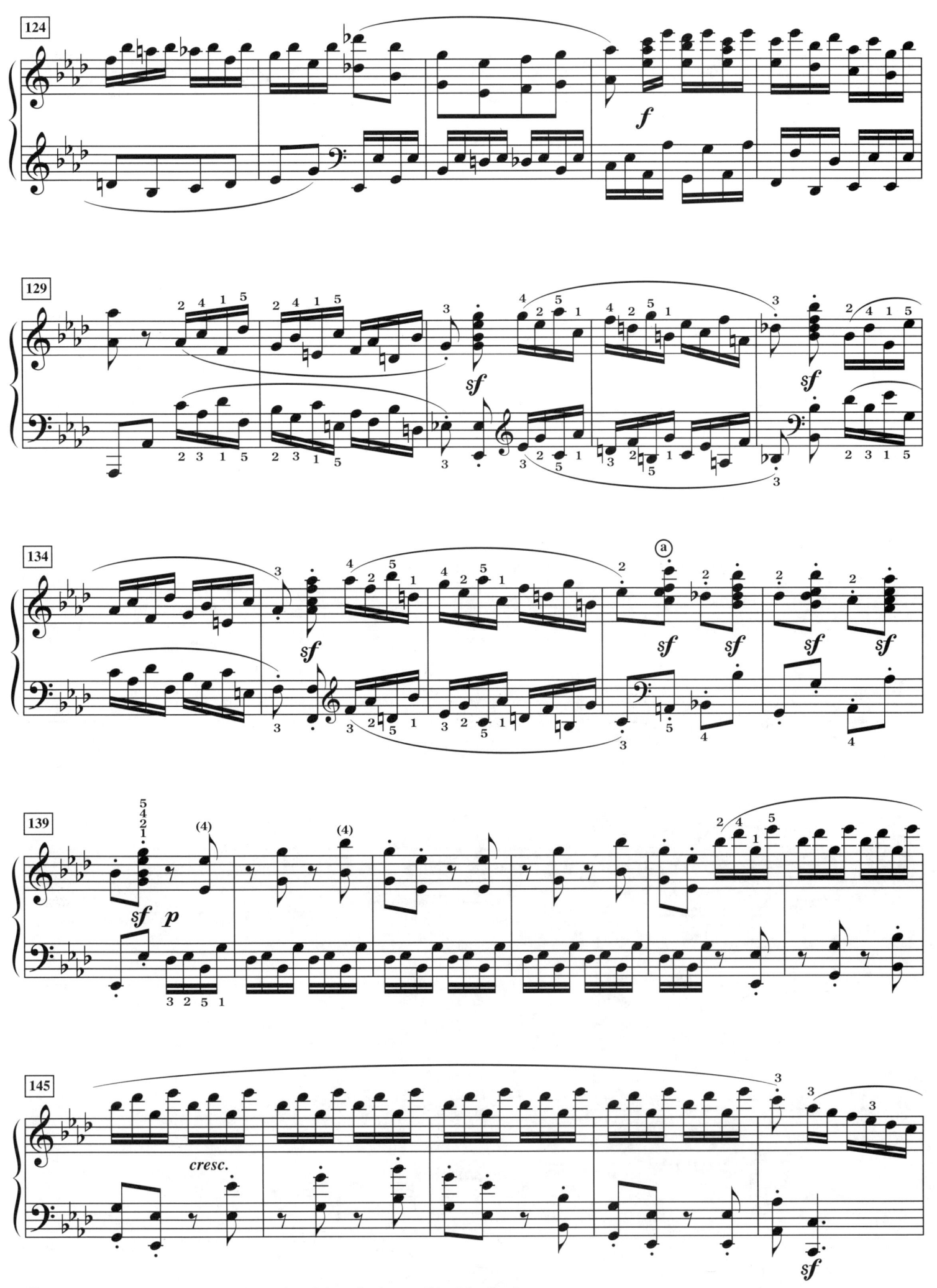

ⓐ Players with small hands may need to delete the lower C in this chord.

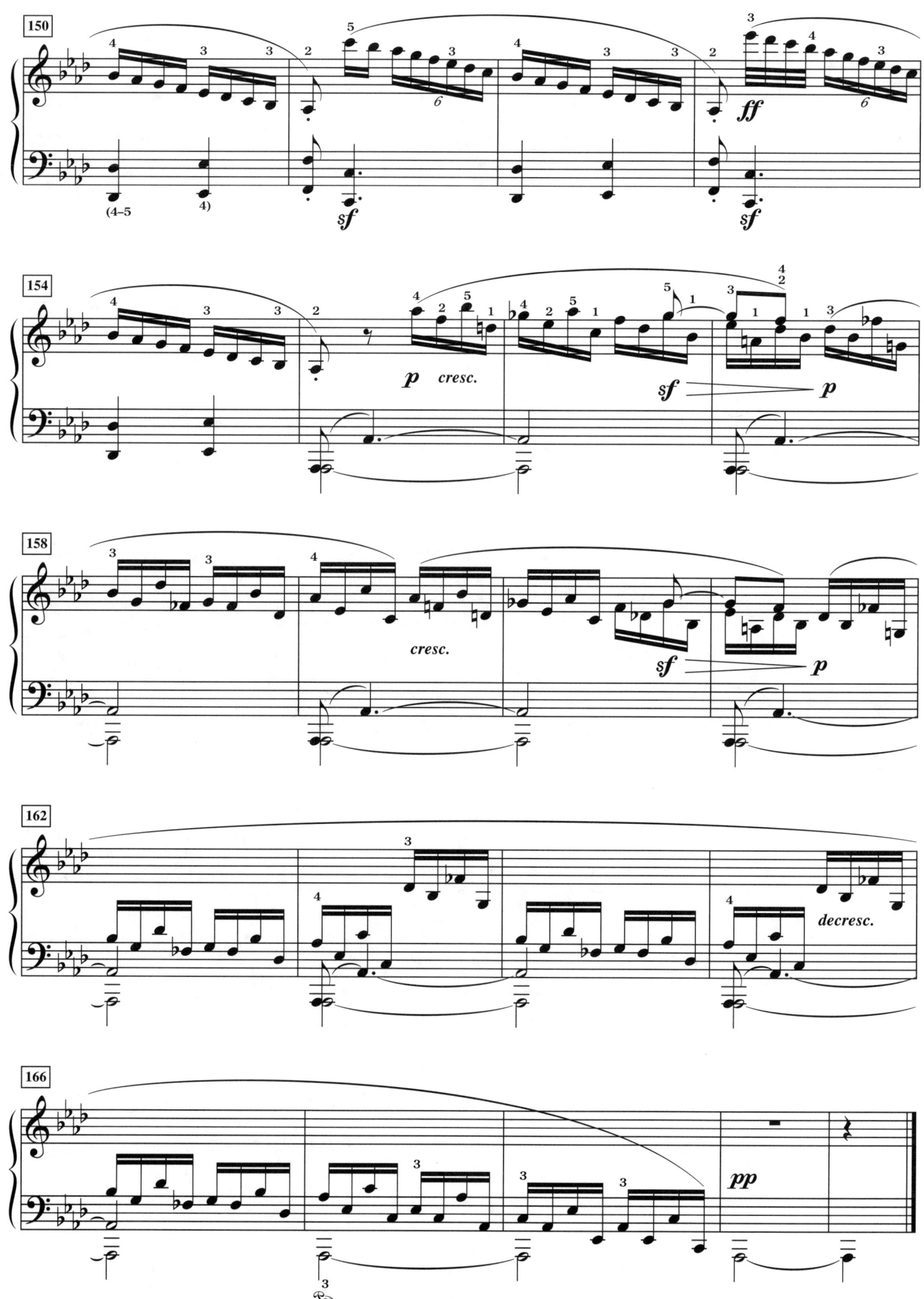

About the Op. 27 Set

The Op. 27 sonatas both carry the indication *Sonata quasi una fantasia*, and, indeed, each in its own way is experimental. Along with the Op. 26 sonata, the set was announced in the *Wiener Zeitung* on March 3, 1802, by Giovanni Cappi. (See "About Op. 26" for more information about Cappi.) The first of the Op. 27 sonatas was dedicated to Princess Josephine von Liechtenstein (1776–1848). Born Countess Josephine Sophie zu Fürstenberg-Weytra, she was married in 1792 to the Prince Johann Joseph von Liechtenstein, a field marshal in the Imperial Army and a famous art collector. Not much has been preserved of Beethoven's relationship with the Princess other than a letter dated September, 1805 (apparently undelivered), in which the composer asks for help for financial assistance for his friend and pupil, Ferdinand Ries.

Beethoven's autograph of Sonata No. 14 in C-sharp Minor, *Op. 27, No. 2, first page of the* Presto agitato *movement*

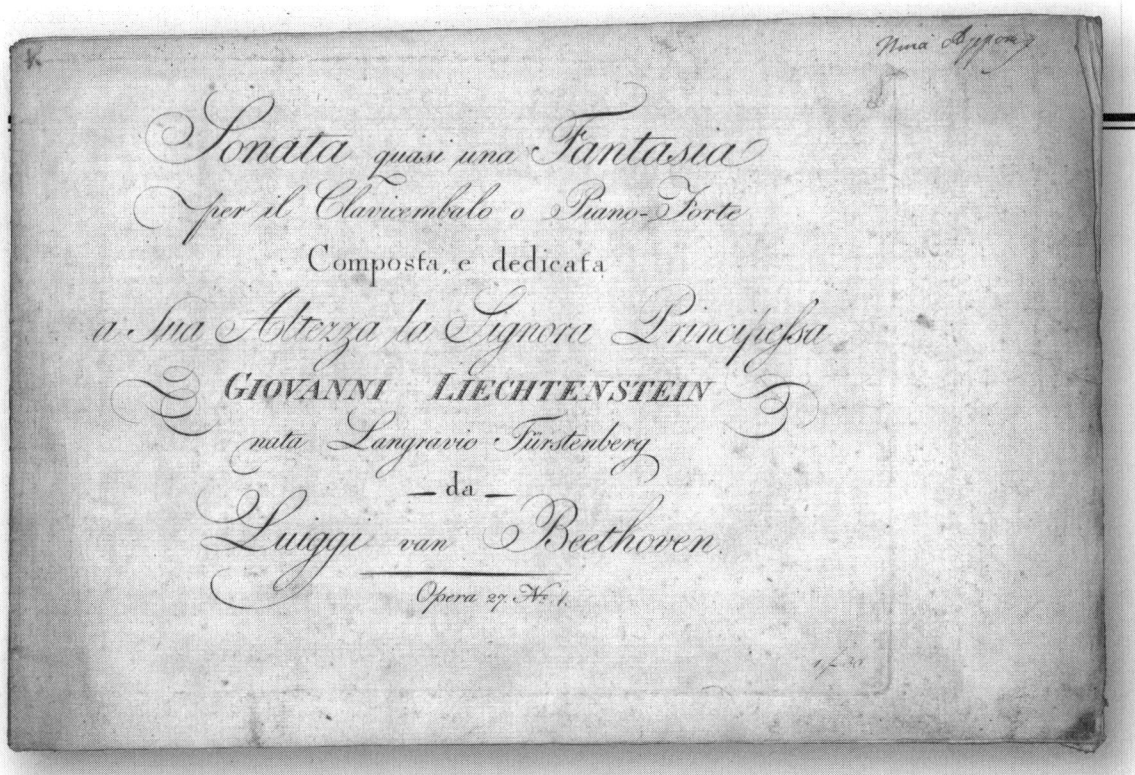

Op. 27, No. 1 title page from the first edition, reproduced by kind permission from the copy in the Austrian National Library, Hoboken Collection, S. H. Beethoven 130

Sonata No. 13 in E-flat Major (Sonata quasi una fantasia), Op. 27, No. 1

Autograph/facsimile:	lost
Sketches/loose pages:	movements 1, 2, and 4
First edition:	Cappi: Vienna, 1802

The Op. 27, No. 1 is to be played without pauses between movements, the composer marking *attacca* between all movements. The first movement avoids sonata-allegro form and substitutes instead a simple **A B A** structure, the outer sections, marked *Andante* in the key of E-flat major, and the middle section in C major, marked *Allegro*. The opening **A** section is itself sectional, presenting three eight-measure sections in its own **A B A** arrangement. The first section (measures 1–9) consists of two sets of four measures, each marked to be repeated, both ending in the tonic. It presents a motive throughout made up of two quarter notes followed by a half note. The second section (measures 10–22) opens in E-flat with a varied statement of the opening theme and stays in that key for its first four measures, marked to be repeated. The next four measures (measures 15–18) open by presenting the varied theme in C major and by moving back to E-flat. The repeat of this section (measures 19–22) is written out to introduce more variation, as are the repeats of the return of the **A** section (measures 23–38). The *Allegro* section is also made up of two eight-measure fragments, the first marked to be repeated (measures 39–46), and the second (measures 47–64) being written out to effect the transition back to the final **A** section (measures 65–80). That section once again presents the opening theme, the repeats of its four-measure units being written out to effect further variation. There is an eight-measure coda (measures 81–88).

As with the Op. 26, the second movement is rapid. Although it is marked simply *Allegro molto e vivace*, it is scherzo-like in spirit. Its structure is clearly that of the scherzo and trio arrangement, the *da capo* being written out to repeat the first of its two sections, introducing a syncopated rhythmic variation at measure 97 that continues to the end of the movement.

The *Adagio con espressione* presents a concise **A B A** arrangement, the **B** section starting at measure 9, and the **A** returning at measure 17. A cadenza is then presented in measure 24 as a bridge to the final movement.

The final *Allegro vivace* is a combination of rondo and sonata-allegro form in the structure **A B A C A B** coda. The return of **A** after the first **B** (measure 82) suggests a rondo, but the fact that the two **B** sections are respectively in the dominant (upbeat to measure 36–81) and tonic (upbeat to measure 204–255), that the **C** section (measures 106–166) focuses on developing the opening theme, and that there is no final return of **A** suggests sonata-allegro form. Instead of the final return of the main theme, the composer unexpectedly introduces a short statement of the opening theme of the *Adagio* (measure 256), now in E-flat. The fact that this section is marked *Tempo I* suggests that perhaps the *Adagio* and the final *Allegro* were conceived as a single movement. Such speculation is, however, mitigated by the composer having written *Attacca subito l'Allegro vivace* at the end of the cadenza leading to the final movement. Since the *attacca* instruction was used between the preceding movements of this work, it might be reasoned that the composer was suggesting that the player move ahead to a fourth movement without a break. If one adopts this interpretation, then the sonata becomes a four movement work, and offers the first example of cyclicism in the sonatas, one that predates by five or six years the first symphonic cyclicism of the Symphony No. 5, Op. 67.

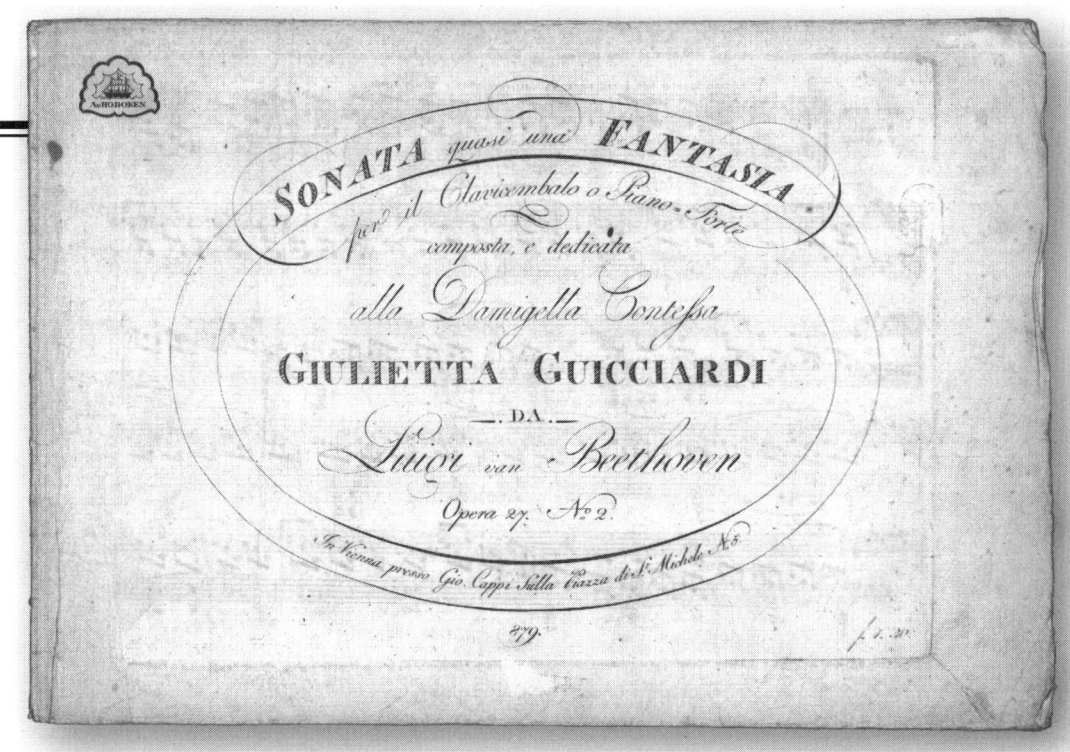

Op. 27, No. 2 title page from the first edition, reproduced by kind permission from the copy in the Austrian National Library, Hoboken Collection, S. H. Beethoven 134

Sonata No. 14 in C-sharp Minor (Sonata quasi una fantasia), Op. 27, No. 2

Autograph/facsimile:	survived except for first and last pages
Sketches/loose pages:	movement 3
First edition:	Cappi: Vienna, 1802

The Op. 27, No. 2 is dedicated to Countess Giulietta Guicciardi (1784–1856), who became a student of Beethoven in 1801. Beethoven was attracted to her, and she likely had a teenage crush on him for a short time. However, in 1803 she married Count Wenzel von Gallenberg (1783–1839). Anton Felix Schindler (1795–1864) claimed in his biography of Beethoven that Giulietta Guicciardi was the object of the famous love letter addressed to the Immortal Beloved found among the composer's papers after his death. More recent research, however, has discredited Schindler's claim.

The nickname "moonlight" probably came from a poetic phrase used to describe the sonata in about 1832. The description was by the poet-musician Heinrich Friedrich Rellstab (1799–1860), who visited Beethoven during a stay in Vienna in April and May of 1825. Rellstab wrote of "a boat passing the wild scenery of Lake Lucerne in the moonlight."[38] The Op. 27, No. 2 is the second of the sonatas for which the autograph is extant, albeit the first and final pages of the work are missing.

The opening movement sustains a mood of serenity throughout, striving for uniformity rather than contrast. Within this context, however, a free sonata-allegro structure can be discerned. The opening theme is stated in the home key of C-sharp minor at the upbeat to measure 6 after a short introduction. At measure 15 a second idea revolves around the dominant of E minor, finally coming to a cadence in F-sharp minor in measure 23, the point at which the "development" begins. This section states the opening theme in F-sharp minor, extends it, and ends with a series of diminished seventh arpeggios. The "recapitulation" begins at the upbeat to measure 43, the second idea now centering on the dominant of F-sharp minor and coming to a close in C-sharp minor at measure 60, ushering in the 10-measure coda that closes the movement. It is not this underlying structure, however, that is at the heart of the music, but rather the unity of mood. In placing emotional content above structure the composer foreshadows a philosophy that is to become a hallmark of 19th-century Romanticism.

The indication *Attacca subito il seguente* is placed at the end of the first movement, so that the following *Allegretto* follows without a break. It is compressed minuet and trio type, the only variation in structure being that the opening section is not marked to be repeated, the composer having written out a repeat of the first eight measures with rhythmic variations. Both the outer sections and the Trio are in the key of D-flat major.

The final movement of this work, *Presto agitato*, is the longest, most dramatic of the three. It is in a sonata-allegro form and stands in strong contrast with the serenity of the first movement. The exposition opens with a first theme of rapid, rising arpeggios. The second theme begins in the dominant minor at measure 21, followed by an extended closing section at measure 43. The exposition is marked to be repeated. The development section (measures 66–102) works with both first and second themes and ends with a section that presents a long tremolo on the dominant of the home key (measures 88–100). The recapitulation (measures 103–157) is regular. A dramatic coda (measures 158–201) makes use of both first and second theme material, adding dramatic cadenza-like passagework (measures 164–167 and 178–190). A final statement of closing theme material (measures 191–196) leads to a burst of arpeggios, bringing the movement and this famous sonata to a brilliant close.

---

[38] Wilhelm von Lenz, *Beethoven et ses trios styles* (Paris: Gustave Legouix, 1909, originally published in 1852), p. 199.

Dedicated to the Princess Josephine von Liechtenstein

Sonata No. 13 in E-flat Major
(Sonata quasi una fantasia)

Ludwig van Beethoven (1770–1827)
Op. 27, No. 1

ⓐ The first edition shows the meter as 𝄵. Some editions, including Schenker, erroneously show 𝄴.

ⓑ The first edition indicates fingering 5-3-1 for the chord on beat 3 of this measure. Using 5-2-1 may be more comfortable for some hands. Of the referenced editors, only Tovey addresses how small hands should deal with the measure if they cannot manage playing the chord solidly. He recommends that the eighth-note accompaniment be played in time and the melody notes follow. This execution he finds preferable to eighth notes played before the beat or arpeggiation. This editor agrees.

(c) The following two arrangements alleviate stretching in this passage:

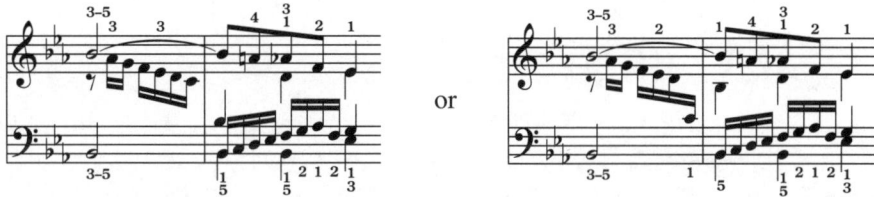

(d) Eight of the referenced editors offer fingering that suggests starting the trills in measures 19 and 20 on the main note. Bülow calls for it in a footnote. Schnabel's fingering specifically calls for a seven-note figure, including two grace notes. Arrau's fingering suggests a six-note figure, starting in each case on the upper note. Tovey also suggests this realization in his notes, but the fingering offered in the music itself (Craxton's perhaps) suggests starting on the main note. This editor likes starting on the main notes using a five-note figure, a realization deemed in keeping with the overall serenity of the section:

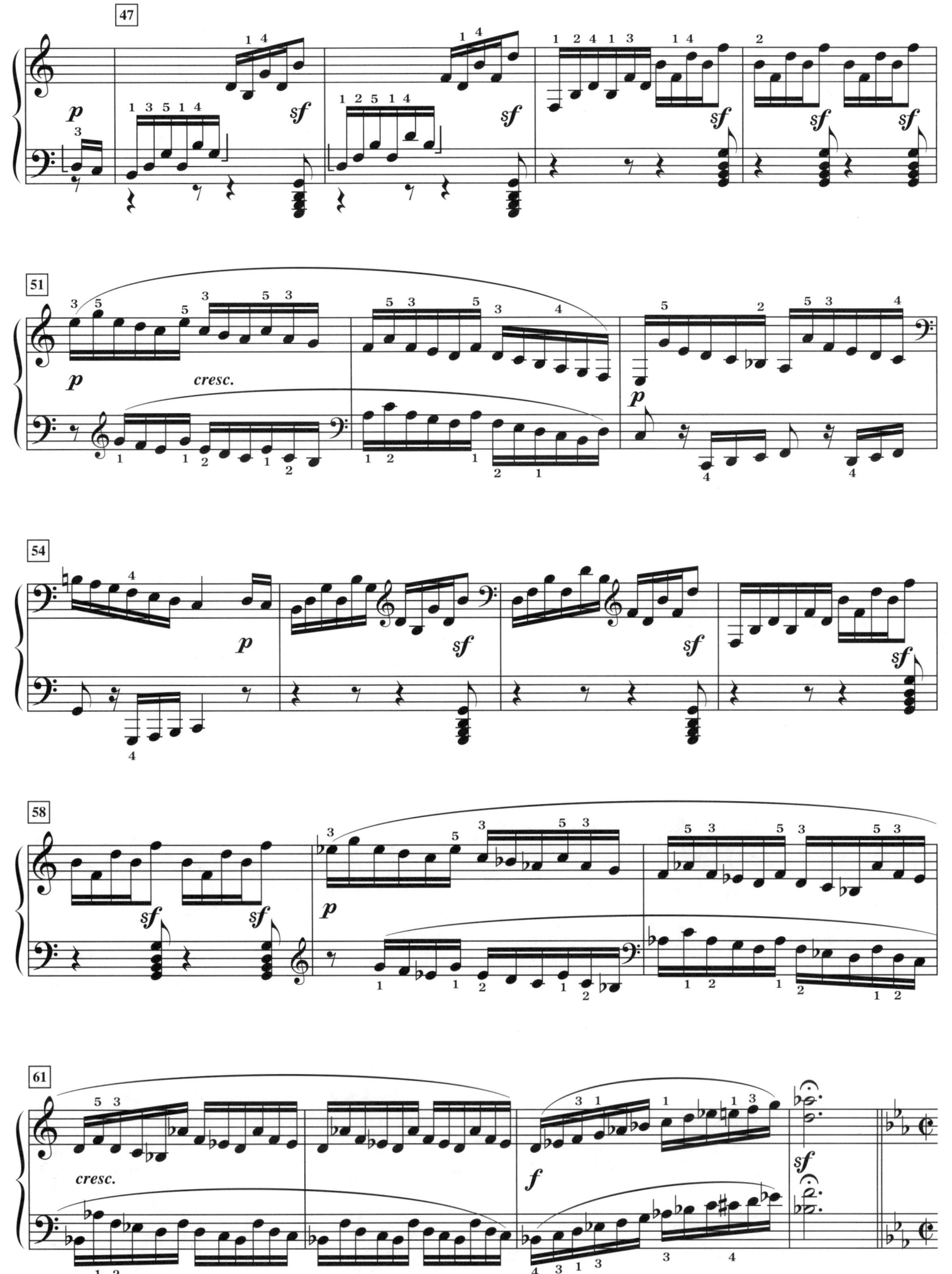

(a) The first edition indicates two identical dynamic markings, one for each hand in the following measures: pick-up to measure 1, measures 17, 19, 43, 45, 79, 97, 113, 133, and 140. Contemporary editorial practice is to use but a single mark in these measures. It is possible that the double markings were meant to indicate a texture born of playing the hands with equal intensity.

ⓑ Ten of the referenced editors offer help with this trill. They all agree that it should start on the main note. Nine editors add closing notes (*nachschlagen*), although none are shown in the first edition. This editor agrees with the consensus, recommending sixteenth notes for measure 54 and the first two beats of measure 55, with a triplet sixteenth incorporating the closing notes on beat 3.

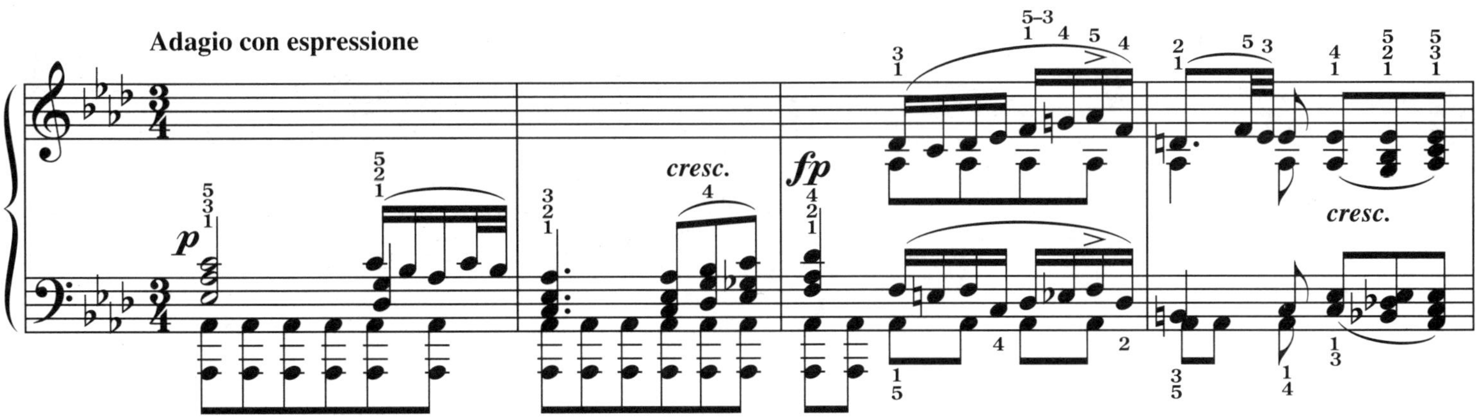

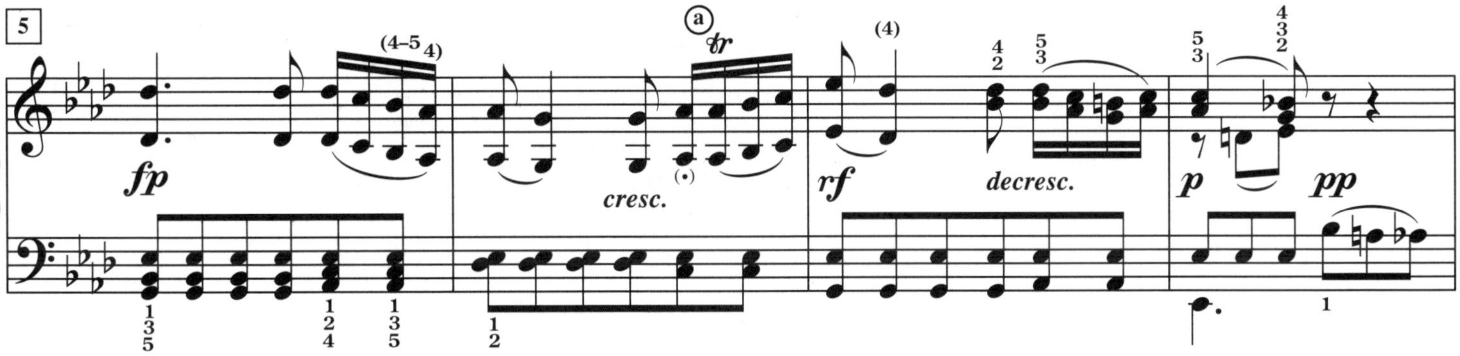

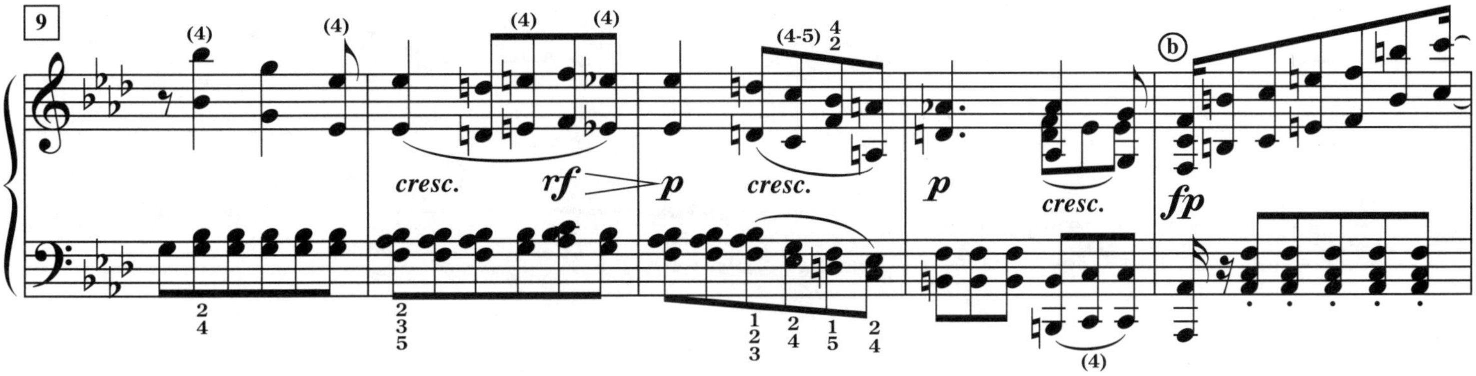

ⓐ Of the referenced editors, seven offer suggestions for this ornament. All agree that the ornament should have closing notes (*nachschlagen*). Five (and this editor) subscribe to a simple turn:

Arrau's fingering suggests a six-note ornament starting on the upper auxiliary. Tovey calls for beginning on the upper note in his written comments for this movement. For those players whose hand is not large enough to manage comfortably, taking one or more of the lower notes of the RH octaves with the LH is an option. These comments also apply to the trills in measures 22 and 23, as well as those in the return of this passage at the end of the *Allegro vivace* (measures 261–262).

ⓑ The first edition shows staccato marks in only the LH in measures 13–15. Seven of the referenced editors add staccato to the LH of measure 16 without comment. Although there is no slur indicated in the RH in the first edition, eight of the editors suggest fingering that strives for a legato line in contrast to the bass. Such fingering always involves playing some octaves with the first and fourth fingers, or substituting fingering on some octaves from 1–5 to 1–4, techniques that performers with small hands may find difficult or impossible. In addition, Bülow and Casella add slurs to the RH in these measures, Casella even creating a LH phrasing pattern for measure 16. Schnabel suggests pedaling on each LH eighth note in this passage, a procedure that some might regard as compromising the staccato indications. This editor agrees that in measures 13–15 a distinctly different touch for each hand is suggested by the first edition. Each performer must decide on the extent to which the RH should or can achieve a completely legato line, based on aesthetic conviction and what is possible for the hand to reach.

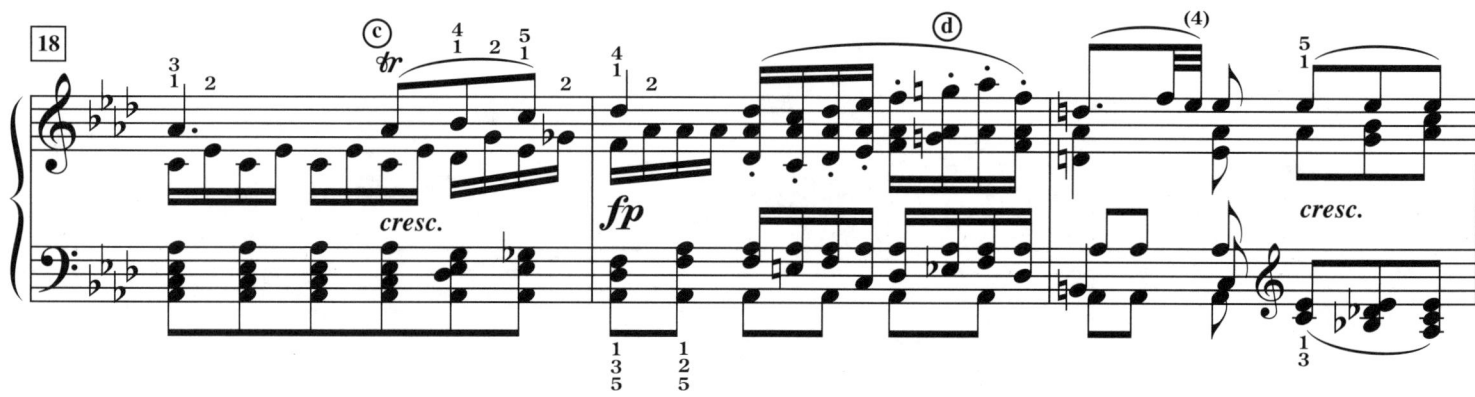

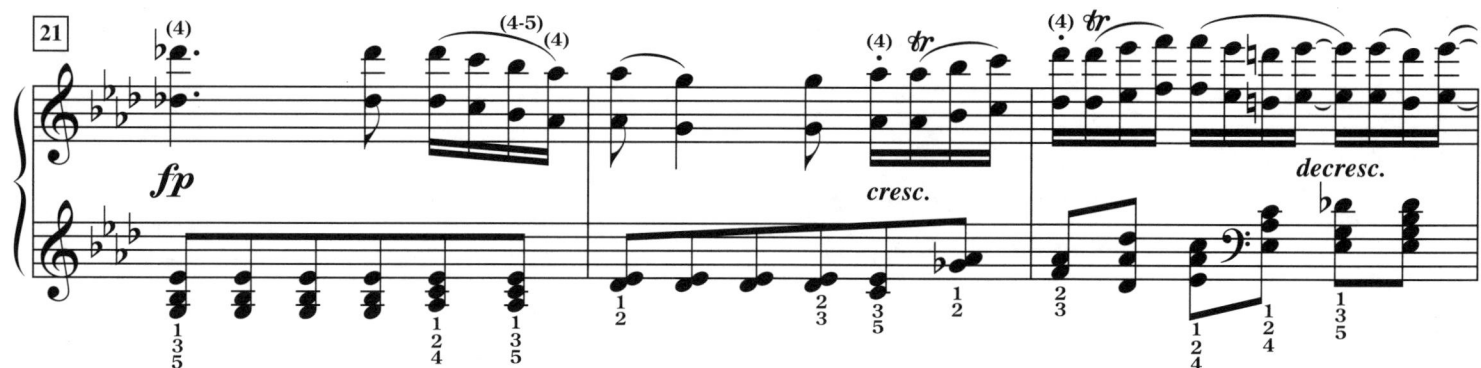

ⓒ Nine of the referenced editors suggest starting this trill on the main note and adding closing notes (*nachschlagen*). Six of these offer detailed realization either through fingering or writing out the ornament in a footnote. Casella and Köhler use a seven-note figure (preferred also by this editor):

Casella and Köhler: d'Albert uses five notes:

Bülow, Schenker, and Schnabel suggest a nine-note ornament, with Schnabel adding his own rhythmic configuration:

Bülow and Schenker: Schnabel:

Tovey's footnote calls for beginning on the upper note, but offers no further realization. Arrau's fingering suggests a six-note figure starting on the upper note:

ⓓ In the opinion of this editor, it is better to leave out one of the lower notes if your hand cannot reach this chord than to try to break it up in any way.

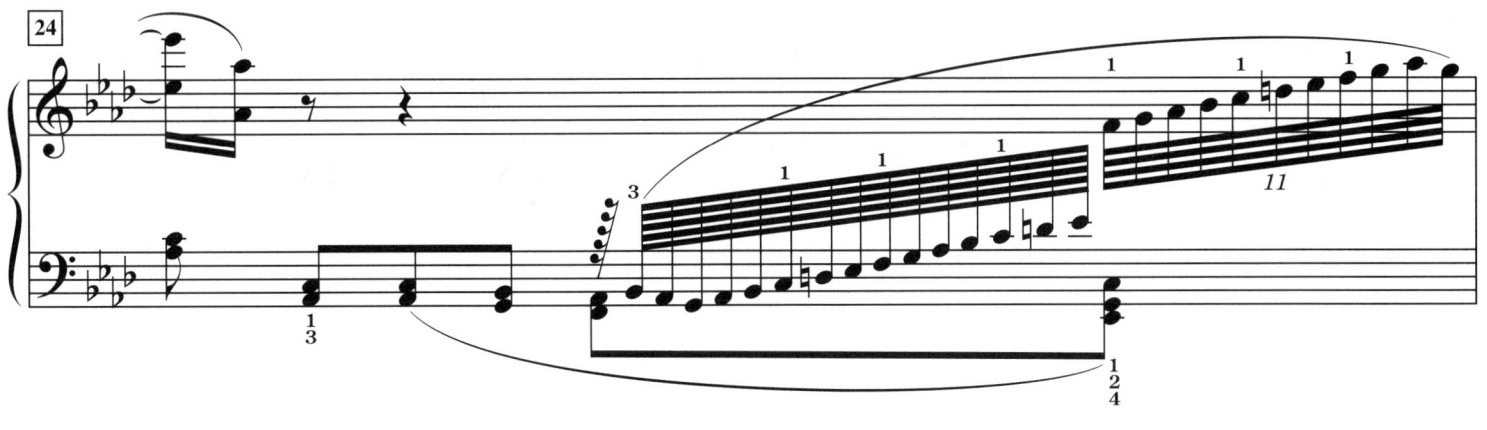

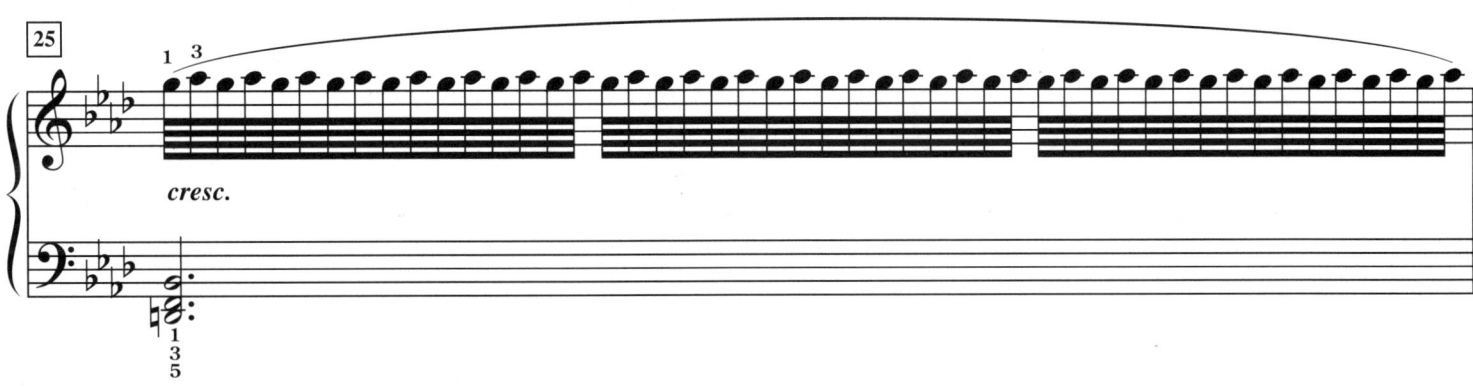

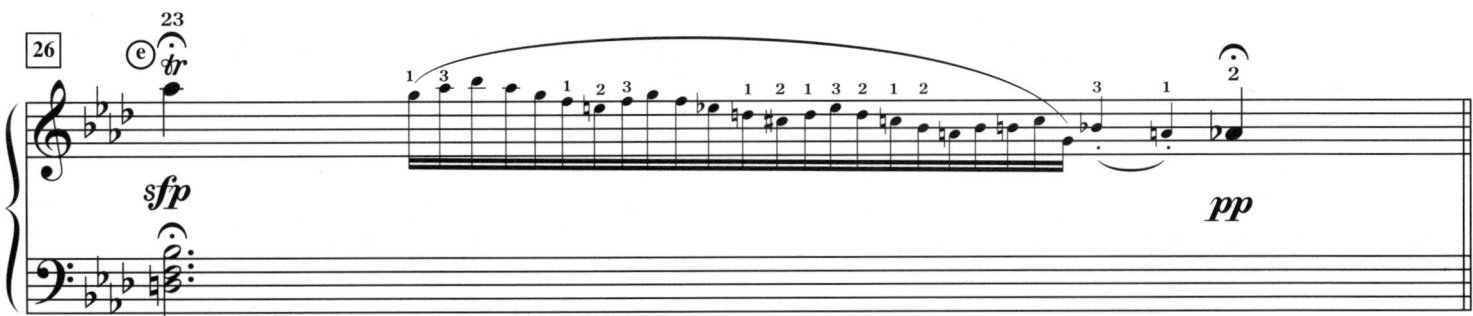

Attacca subito l'Allegro vivace

(e) The improvisatory nature of this passage has led to a variety of suggestions from nine of the referenced editors. D'Albert, Casella, Geoffroy, Schenker, and Schnabel start the trill on the main note. This editor agrees, believing that emphasizing the seventh of the dominant harmony in E-flat is important in this transition back to the home key of the sonata. Bülow and Tovey add a B-flat grace note before the trill, not indicating if this addition is to be played before the downbeat or on it. Köhler adds a similar grace note on G. Arrau's fingering suggests starting the trill on the upper note.

Bülow, Schnabel, and Tovey each suggest a way of dividing up the ensuing cadenza. Bülow places accents on the third, ninth, fifteenth, and twenty-first notes of the cadenza, cautioning the performer not to make them too heavy. Tovey suggests a division of 8+8+7. Schnabel's rendition works well, but it has also taken the broadest liberties with the original notation:

Allegro vivace

(ⓐ) Ten of the referenced editors offer suggestions for executing this ornament. All start on the main note. Only Arrau, Bülow, and Casella indicate the extent of the ornament, but tempo and rhythm pretty much dictate the five-note figure they recommend:

The closing notes (*nachschlag*) are indicated in the first edition. Schnabel and Tovey offer an easier version as a possibility:

These ideas may also be applied to the trills in measures 6, 83, 87, 168, and 172.

ⓑ The LH should be over the RH starting from the upbeat of measure 36. At about measure 51 the positioning of the hands will need to be adjusted. Geoffroy, Schenker, and Wallner suggest shifting the LH under the RH on the downbeat of measure 51. Arrau and Casella recommend shifting on beat 2 of that measure. Tovey's solution, attractive to this editor, is to take the LH G on the downbeat of measure 51 with finger 2 of the RH, thereby giving the LH ample time to reposition under the RH. D'Albert, Bülow, Köhler, and Martienssen start fingering the LH skips of an octave with 2 and 5 from beat 2 of measure 50 through measure 52, a solution this editor finds risky.

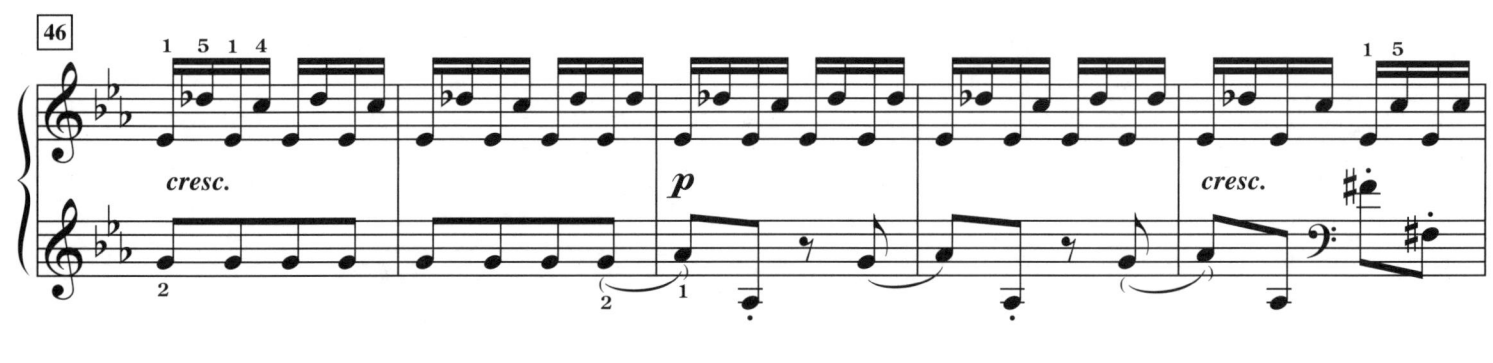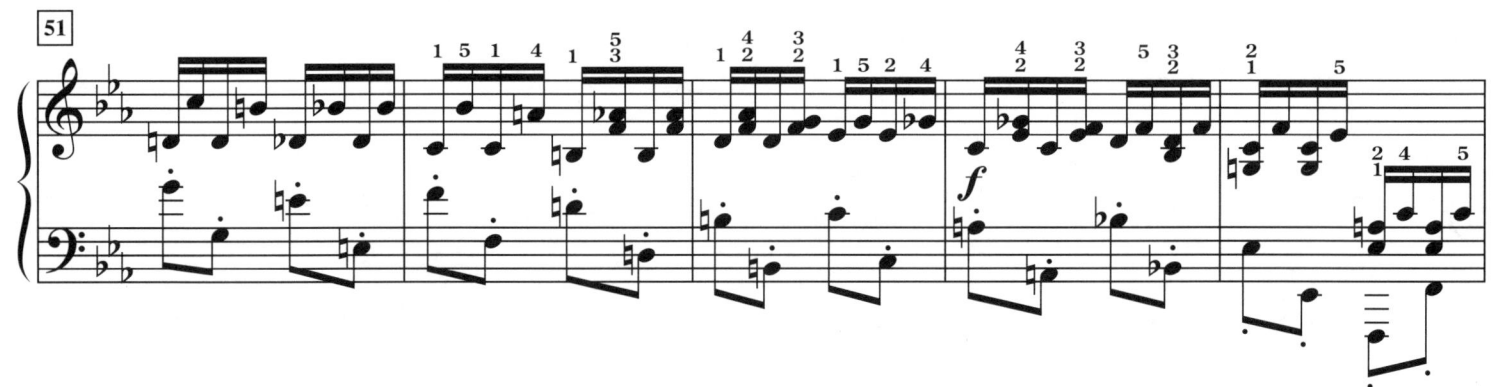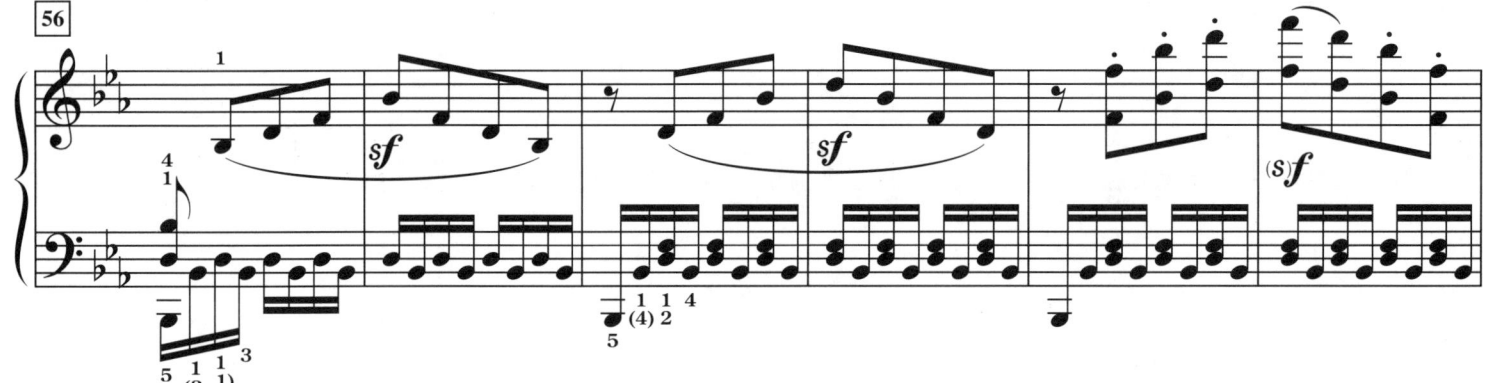

(c) The seven referenced editors who indicate fingering for this trill all start on the main note. At tempo, triplet sixteenths seem to work best with four thirty-seconds on beat 4, incorporating the closing notes:

A similar realization may be applied to the trill in measures 165–166, although the closing notes are absent in the first edition.

(d) Probably erroneously, the first edition shows the following:

(e) Solutions as to the relative positioning of the hands in measures 218–221 are different from those in measures 51–52, due to the different physical relationship with the black and white keys. Arrau, Casella, Geoffroy, Schenker, and Wallner indicate shifting the LH under the RH on beat 2 of measure 218, an easy shift since the LH is moving from black keys to white keys. A second problem develops, however, on the downbeat of measure 220. Only Arrau, Casella, Schenker, and Schnabel offer help here, suggesting the LH now get back up over the RH, also fairly easy as the LH now moves from white keys up to black keys. Schenker alone recommends the LH shift back under the RH on beat 2 of measure 220, a difficult and unnecessary shift in the opinion of this editor. Curiously, Tovey, who had provided a clever solution for the passage at measures 51–52, denies any problem exists in the recapitulation! D'Albert, Bülow, Köhler, and Martienssen, once again suggest fingering the LH skips of an octave with 2 and 1, as risky a solution here, in the opinion of this editor, as it was in the earlier passage.

ⓕ See footnote ⓐ for the *Adagio con espressione* movement and adapt it here.

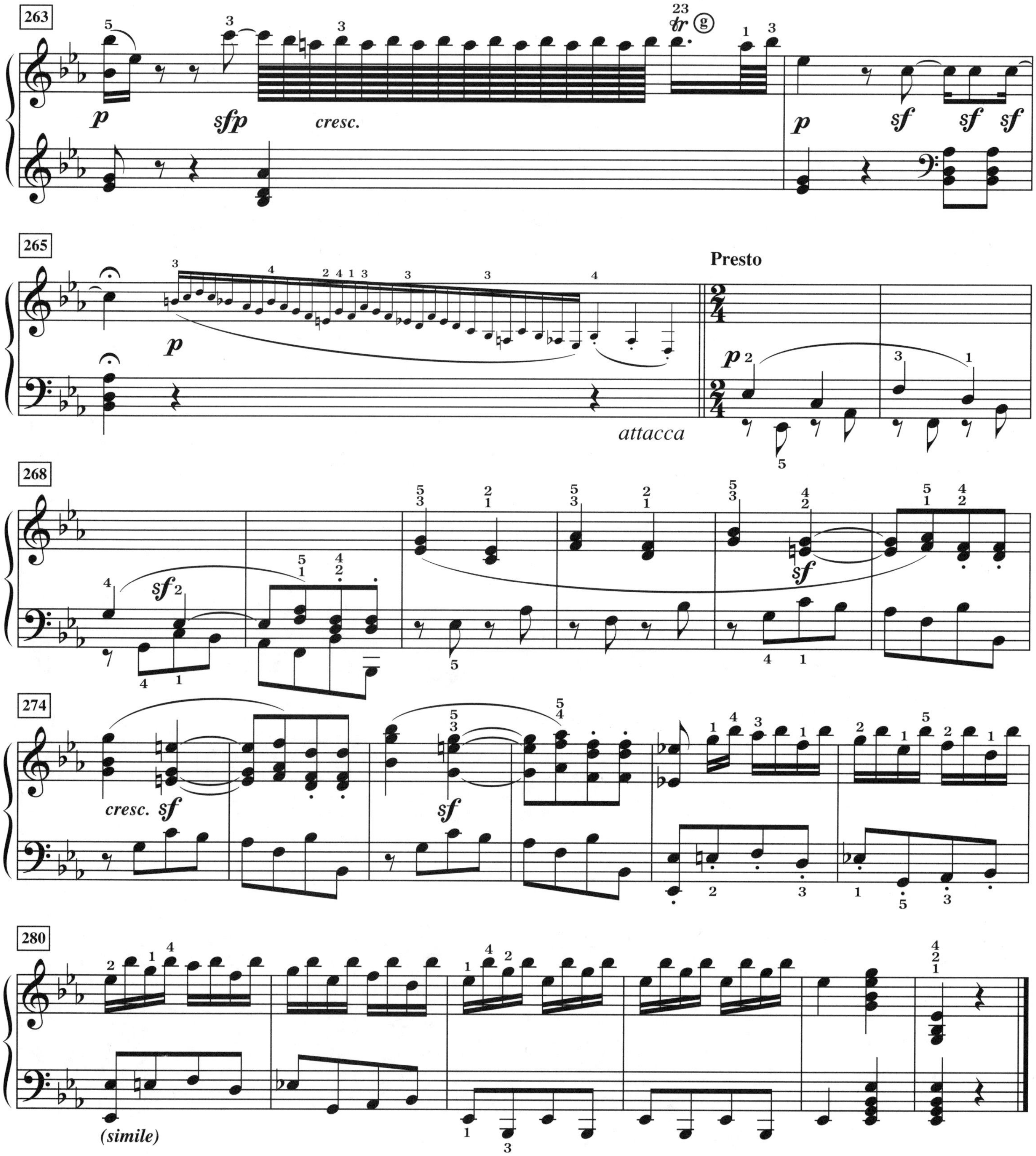

(g) As in the earlier passage in the *Adagio con espressione*, some of the referenced editors offer diverse opinions as to performance. Fingering that suggests starting the B-flat trill on the main note is offered by d'Albert, Casella, Geoffroy, Schenker, and Schnabel. Arrau, Bülow, and Wallner indicate starting on the upper note, Bülow writing in the upper auxiliary C as a grace note. The cadenza that follows in measure 265 is presented clearly in the first edition as twenty-nine grace notes, followed by three quarter notes. Geoffroy, Schenker, and Wallner (as well as this editor) follow the first edition. The other nine of the referenced editors print a thirty-two-note version of the grace-note group, the fifth, sixth, and seventh notes being repeated an extra time.

first edition version:

etc.

some editors' version:

etc.

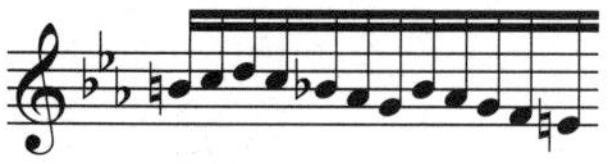

Although Bülow, Schnabel, and Tovey offer suggestions for subdividing the cadenza, these ideas are based on the extended version of the cadenza and would not work with the first edition cadenza.

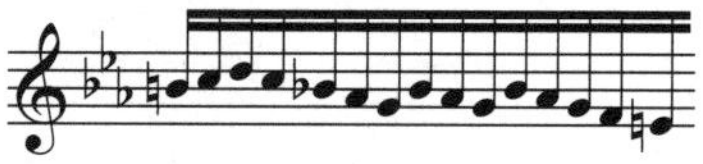

Dedicated to the Countess Giulietta Guiccardi

Sonata No. 14 in C-sharp Minor
(Sonata quasi una fantasia)

Ludwig van Beethoven (1770–1827)
Op. 27, No. 2

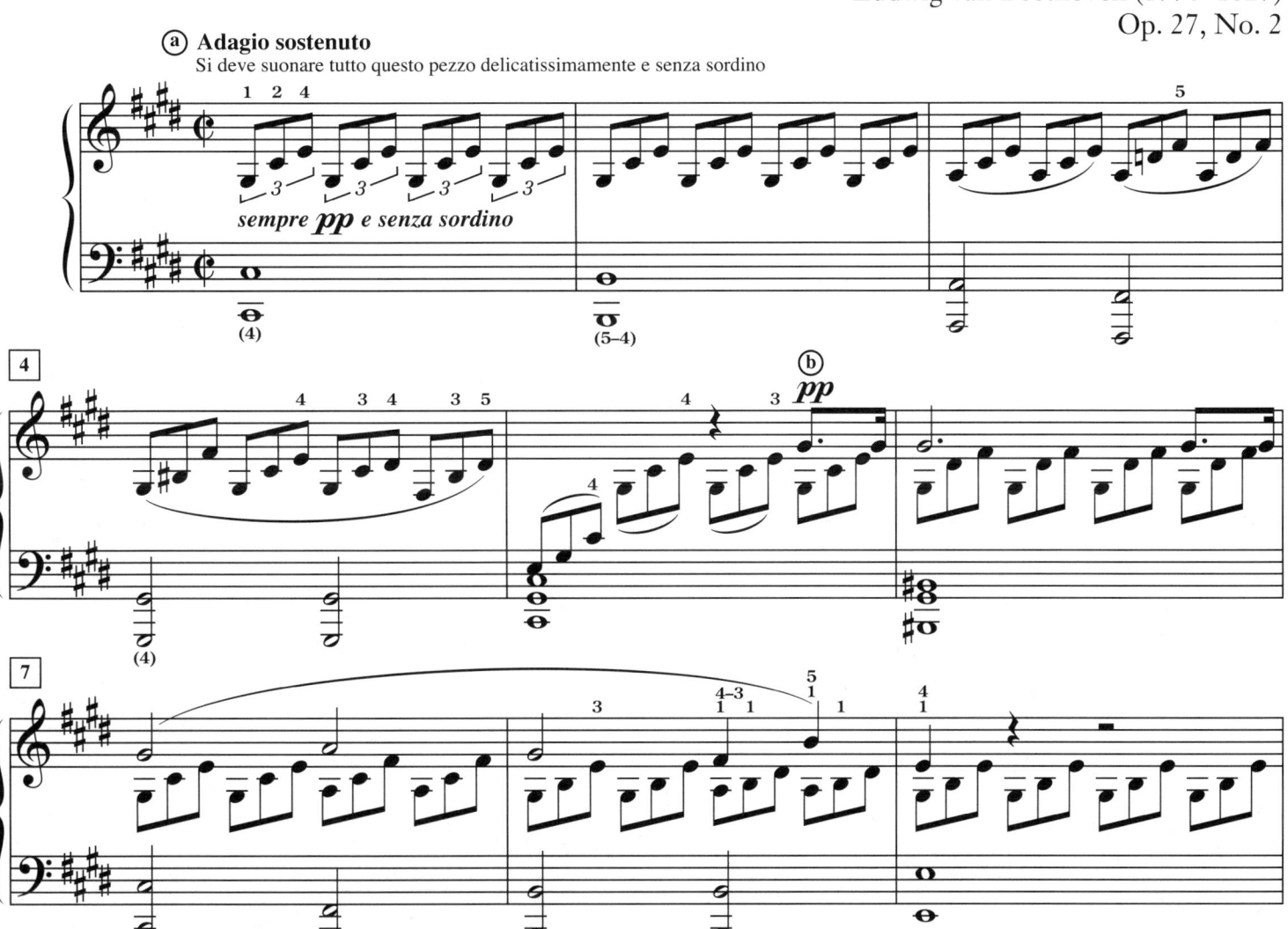

ⓐ Beethoven's directions in Italian state that "this piece should be played throughout with the greatest delicacy and without dampers" (i.e., with pedal). He repeats the "*senza sordino*" (without dampers) direction in measure 1. These directions have been the source of much speculation. Some performers have assumed that the composer meant to direct using the pedal throughout the piece, but with the usual pedal changes whenever the harmony changed. Czerny suggests this as the "prescribed pedal." Others believe Beethoven's directions indicate his interest in creating a special pedal effect. The composer's taste for using harmonic blurring as a coloristic device shows up fairly often in his piano writing: Op. 31, No. 2, first movement; Op. 53, last movement, to mention two famous examples, as well as in the second, third, and fifth piano concertos. It is probable that such effects were possible and attractive on the piano of Beethoven's time. Many performers using today's piano experiment with half-damping, delayed damping, or holding notes down longer than their written value attempting to simulate the effect they believe Beethoven had in mind. British musician Howard Ferguson (1908–1999) suggested depressing the lowest seven keys on the piano keyboard before the movement is to be played, catching them with the sostenuto (middle) pedal, and holding it throughout the movement while pedaling normally with the damper (right) pedal. (Howard Ferguson: *Keyboard Interpretation*, Oxford University Press, New York and London, 1975, p. 163.)

ⓑ The tradition of separating the sixteenth note from the triplet figure is so well established in this movement that no one would suggest applying the early performance practice of assimilating the sixteenth into the last note of the triplet. Moreover, present-day performance practice is mostly supported by the configuration of notes in the first edition, wherein all the sixteenth notes are placed after the last note of the triplet, except for measures 42, 43, 46, and 47, where the sixteenth erroneously appears before the last note of the triplet figure. Beethoven's autograph agrees for the most part. (It should be noted that the first and last pages of the autograph of this work are missing.) Since the composer often used repeat signs for the triplet figure, the triplet/sixteenth-note configuration is represented fully only in measures 23, 42, 46, 62, 63, and 64. The sixteenth appears after the triplet in all these cases except in measure 46, where the sixteenth and the triplet might be read as the interval of a third, and in measure 63, where the composer, perhaps in haste, compresses the group of notes in beat 4 and the sixteenth ends up between the second and third notes of the triplet. Thus, in this sonata the composer's intentions are relatively clear, in contrast to earlier examples. (See Vol. I: Op. 2, No. 2, fourth movement, footnote ⓕ on page 66, and Op. 13, second movement, footnote ⓕ on page 234.)

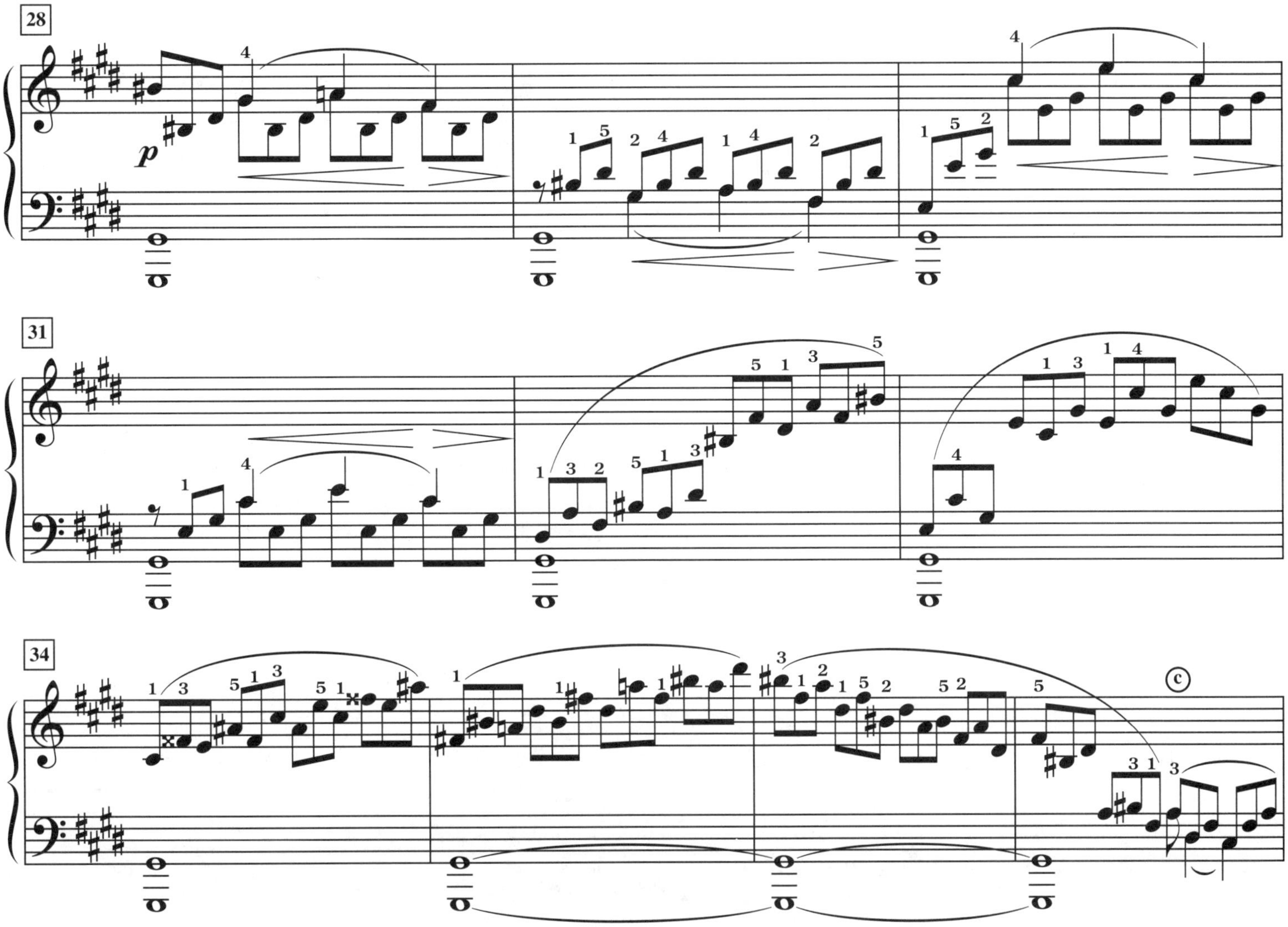

ⓒ Confusion attends the slurring of the notes marked with extra stemming in measures 37–40. First, it is difficult to account for the eighth note downward stem on the first note of the triplet on beat 3 of measure 37. If intended to be a part of the ensuing melodic fragment, then the melody opens with a tri-tone moving from A down to a lower D-sharp. This seems an unlikely interval with which to start a melodic fragment, and including it as part of the melody introduces a pattern that does not match the fragments in measures 38 and 39. Thus, this editor believes that the stemming on the A is for harmonic reinforcement only, and not intended to be part of the melodic pattern.

A second issue is the length of the patterns that are marked in measures 37, 38, and 39. The first edition marks the last two sets of triplets in measure 37 with a single slur, not indicating any additional slurring for the D-sharp and C-sharp with quarter-note stems. In measures 38 and 39, however, the notes marked with quarter-note stems are treated as two-note slurs (D-sharp to C-sharp in measure 38; D-natural to C-sharp in measure 39). Of the referenced editors, Arrau, Geoffroy, Schenker, and Wallner (1952) follow the first edition. Martienssen and Wallner (1980) do also except for adding an additional two-note slur to the stemmed quarter notes in measure 37 (D-sharp and C-sharp). The autograph is not as consistent as the first edition. In measure 37, the composer writes two slurs for the second half of the measure, one over the two sets of triplets and the other under, presumably to be applied to the two stemmed quarter notes. In measures 38 and 39, the only slurs shown are those that apply to the stemmed quarter notes. In measure 38, the slur ends after the last triplet, perhaps suggesting a longer phrase, but measure 39 is at the beginning of a new line and there is no indication of the slur ending on its downbeat. In measure 39, the slur line extends across the bar line into measure 40, although it does not quite reach the stemmed half-note B-sharp. This presentation has led some editors to believe the stemmed notes represent a three-note phrase. Of the referenced editors, Köhler and Schnabel mark three-note phrases across bar lines between measures 37–38, 38–39, and 39–40, thus making the three phrases consistent. Bülow and Tovey inexplicably indicate three-note phrases starting in measure 37 and 38, but show no phrase mark for the stemmed quarter notes in measure 39. This editor believes the autograph shows two-note slurs in measures 37 and 38, and that the slur beginning in measure 39 extends to the downbeat of measure 40. Thus, the composer altered the third repetition of the phrase in two ways: by changing the D-sharp to D-natural as well as extending the phrase to the downbeat of measure 40.

measure 37:

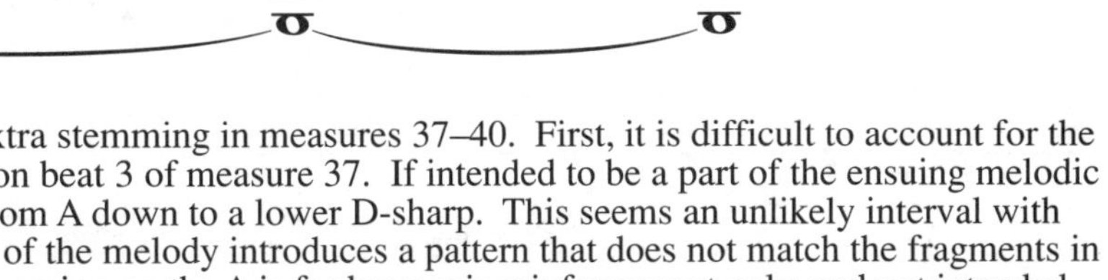

measure 38:

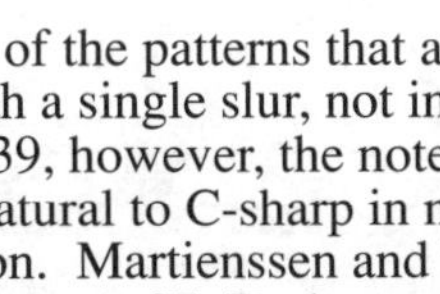

measure 39:

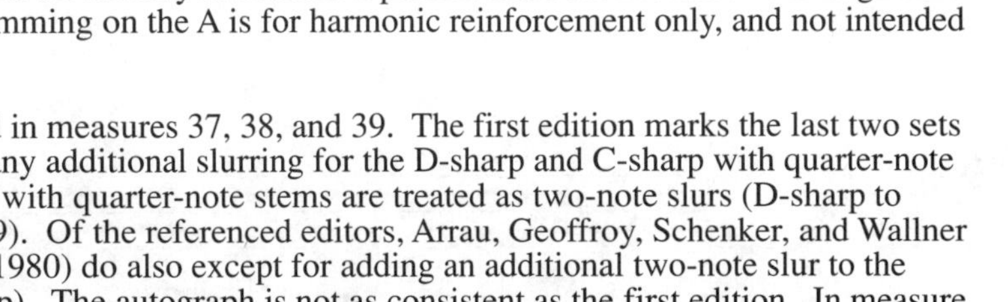

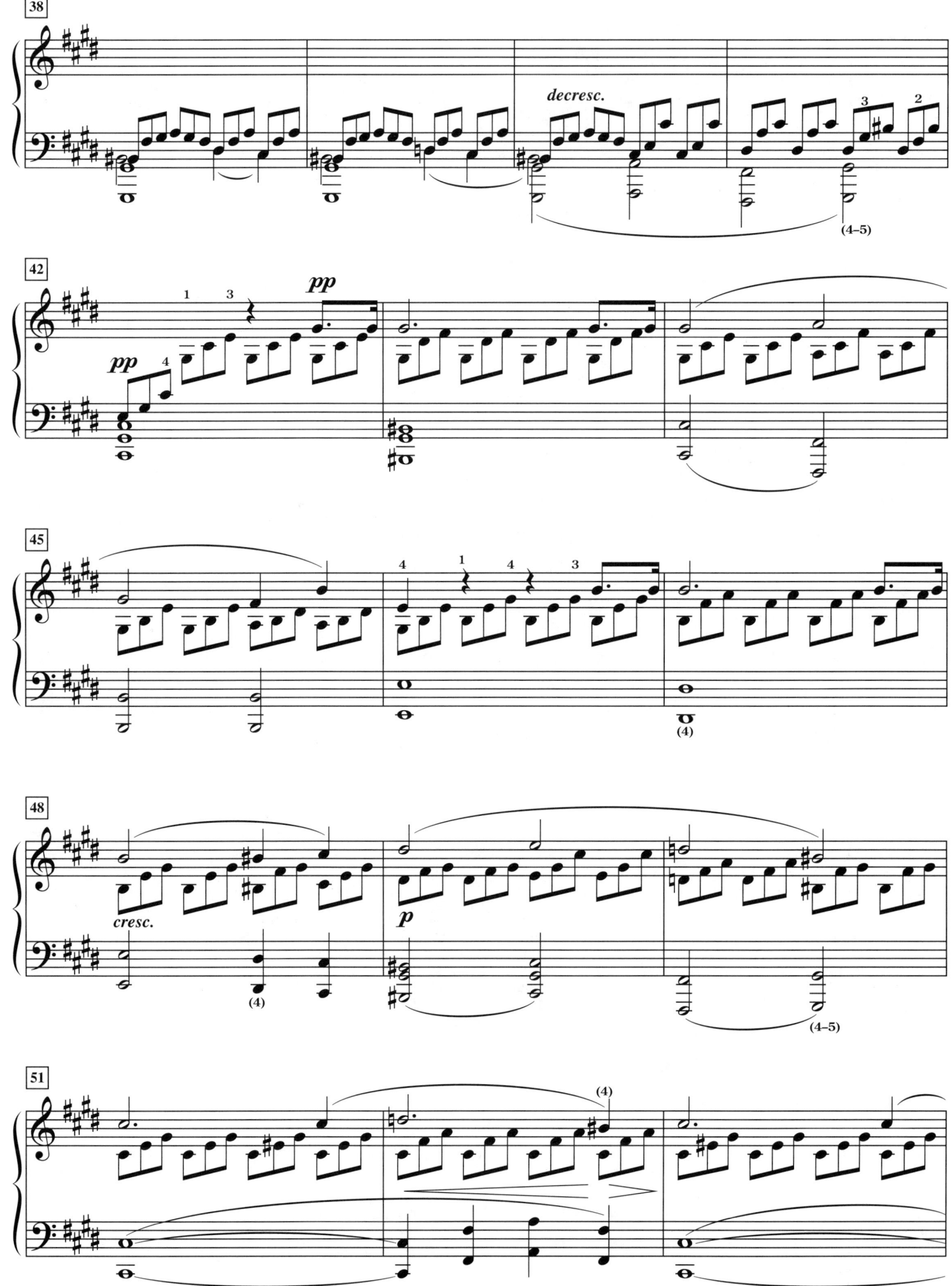

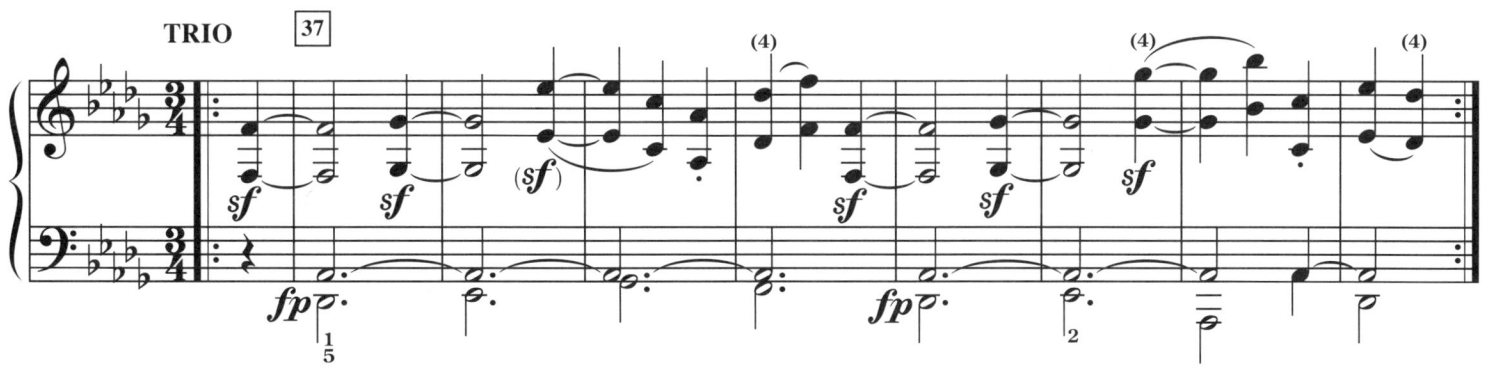
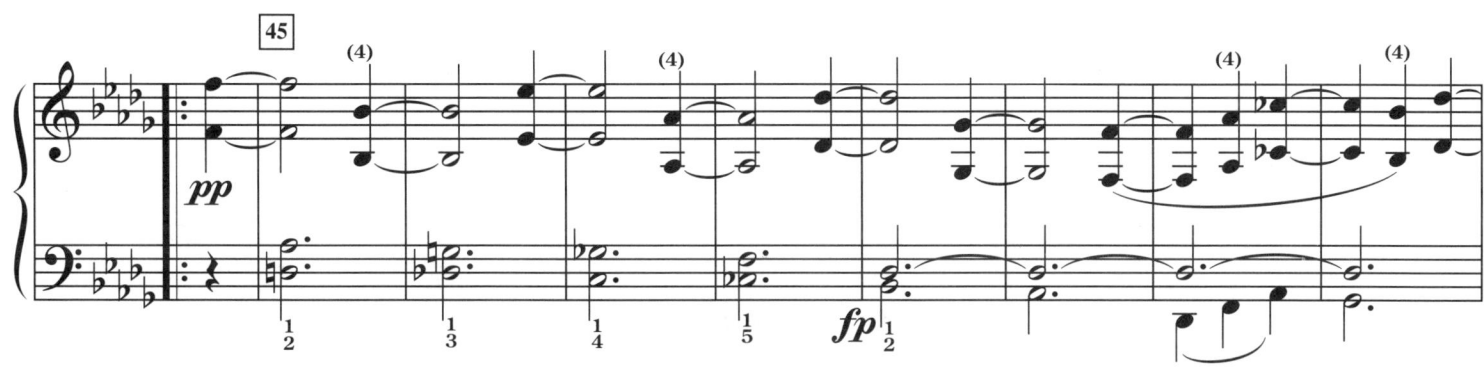
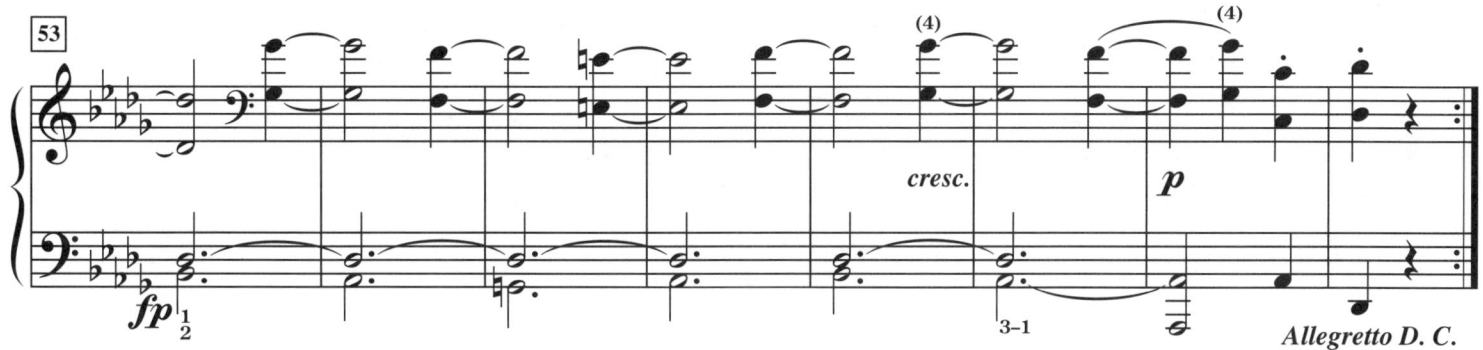
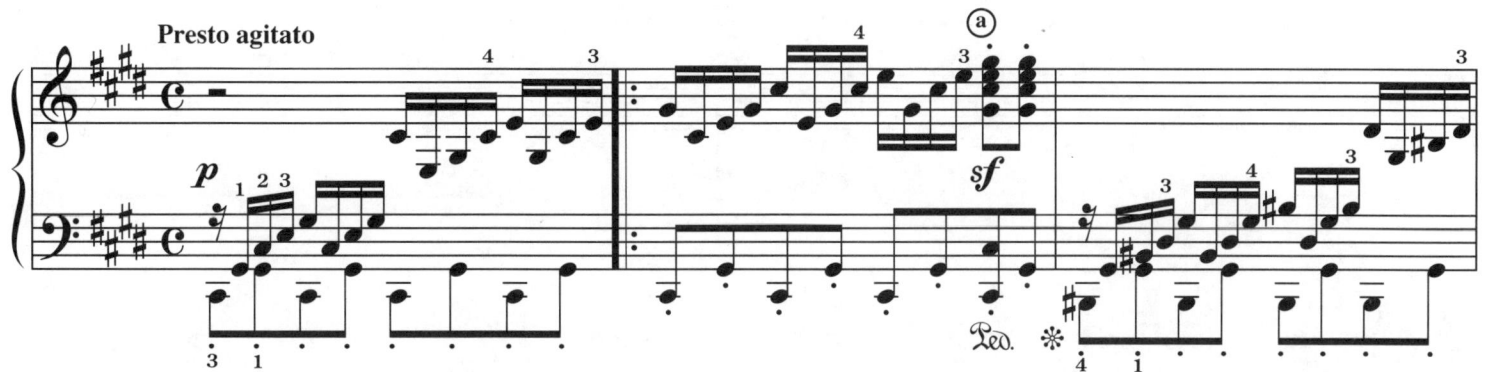

(a) Throughout this movement, the composer's autograph and the first edition consistently indicate *senza sordino* (without dampers, i.e., with pedal) each time the two chords close this passage, as well as writing *con sordino* (with dampers, i.e., without pedal) at each new onset of arpeggiated sixteenth notes. Moreover, these chords often exhibit articulation signs that look to be stronger signs than staccato marks. Articulation symbols are shown in only about two-thirds of the measures that contain these motivic chords, but whenever they appear they resemble wedges or vertical lines rather than dots. These signs appear in measures 4, 6, 8, 67, 69, 70, 71, 104, 106, 108, and 110. They are absent from measures 2, 7, 16, 18, 109, 161, and 163, presumably oversights resulting from the composer's hasty notation. In the first edition these motivic chords are marked with dots of varying thickness throughout the movement.

ⓑ Of the referenced editors, only Bülow and Tovey address the execution of this ornament, both suggesting rapid on-the-beat execution. This editor agrees with their realizations, which can be applied as well to measures 73 and 118.

ⓒ Most editors recommend and most pianists will find that a simple turn works best in this measure and measures 32, 126, and 128:

measure 30:

Arrau recommends and Geoffroy offers as an alternative a seven-note figure, possible but difficult at tempo.

Tovey devises a facilitation for small hands:

measure 30:

ⓓ The fact that the recapitulation presents a different pattern of sixteenth notes in measure 131 has led Casella, Köhler, and Tovey to assume the composer simply ran out of notes on the keyboard of his time, and to admit the possibility of altering the pattern in this measure to match that of the later measure. This editor joins those who eschew such changes, arguing that Beethoven solved the limitations of keyboard range in a specific way and that his solution should be respected.

ⓔ Most editors add closing notes to this trill, inasmuch as both the autograph and the first edition show them in measure 132. Fingering indications of d'Albert, Casella, Köhler, Schnabel, Schenker, and Tovey reflect starting on the main note. Those of Arrau, Geoffroy, and Wallner reflect starting on the upper note. Bülow adds an upper auxiliary grace note before the beat. No one addresses how many notes might be appropriate. This editor likes the following realization:

ⓕ The autograph shows the *p* indication close to the downbeat of measure 43. One might argue that the composer's hand slipped a little, for the indication is just barely to the right of the downbeat, and that it was meant to be applied to the second eighth note. In measure 138, however, such an assumption is not possible because the mark appears to the left of the eighth notes that come on the downbeat. The first edition places the *p* on the second eighth note in measure 43 and before the downbeat in measure 138. Arrau, Geoffroy, and Wallner (1952) follow the first edition without comment. Wallner (1980) moves the dynamic mark to the second eighth note in the text, footnoting where it is in early sources. Eight of the referenced editors move the *p* to the second eighth note in both measures, thus bringing these two measures into conformity with the dynamic patterns of measures 49–53 and 144–148. Casella makes the case in a footnote that the *p* should take effect on the downbeats of both measures 43 and 138. This editor agrees with his reading of the autograph.

(g) Five of the referenced editors address how to play the sixteenth grace notes that appear in measures 59, 61, 62, 92, 96, 98, 154, 156, 157, 193, 195, 196, and 197. Bülow, Casella, Köhler, and Tovey recommend playing the first of the grace notes on the beat with the LH. This editor agrees. Schnabel's indications are sometimes on the beat, sometimes before the beat. He suggests playing on the beat for measures 59; beat 1 of measure 61; measures 92, 96, 98, and 154; beat 1 of measure 156; measure 193; and beat 1 of measure 195. He recommends playing them before the beat for beat 3 of measure 61; measure 62; beat 3 of measure 156; measure 157; beat 3 of measure 195, and measure 196.

(h) Beethoven's autograph shows a crescendo here. It is absent from the first edition.

ⓘ The passage from measure 92 through measure 97 is often cited as an example of the composer's use of two types of articulation in close proximity: the wedge (vertical line) and the dot. The autograph shows thick dots on the last three eighth notes of measure 92 and the first eighth note in measure 93. These dots seem to thicken for the three-note chords starting on the second eighth of measure 93 through measure 94. These wedge-like marks stand in contrast to the dots used under the slur in measure 97. Even in this passage, however, questions remain regarding the composer's intentions, for the two half notes in measure 95 are marked differently, the first with a dot and the second with a wedge.

measures 91–99:

ⓙ The G-sharp in this chord appears in both the autograph and the first edition.

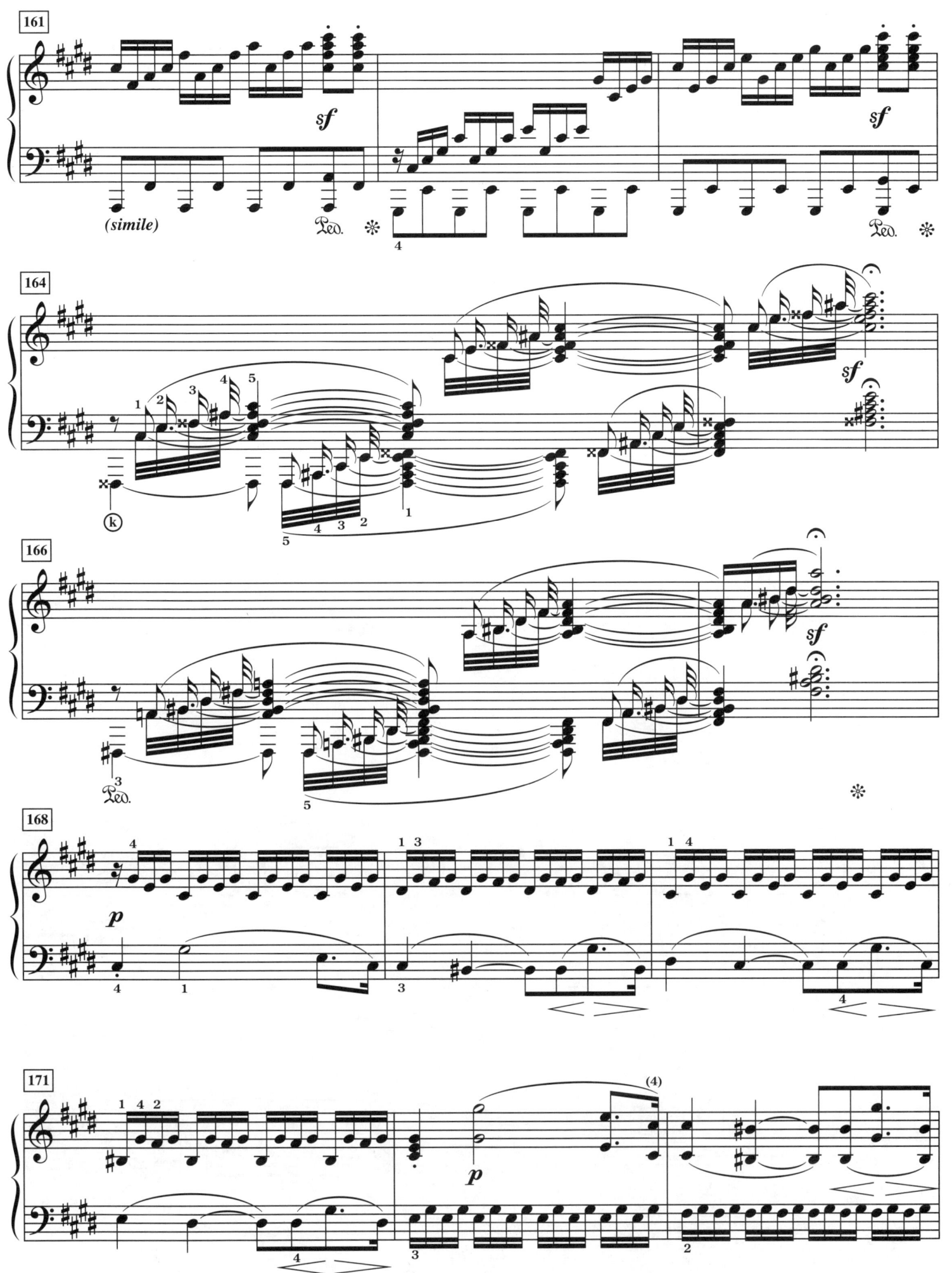

ⓚ In measures 164–165, the composer indicated *con sordino* (without pedal) in contrast to *senza sordino* (with pedal) in measures 167–167. The first edition indicates *con sordino* for the entire passage (measures 164–167).

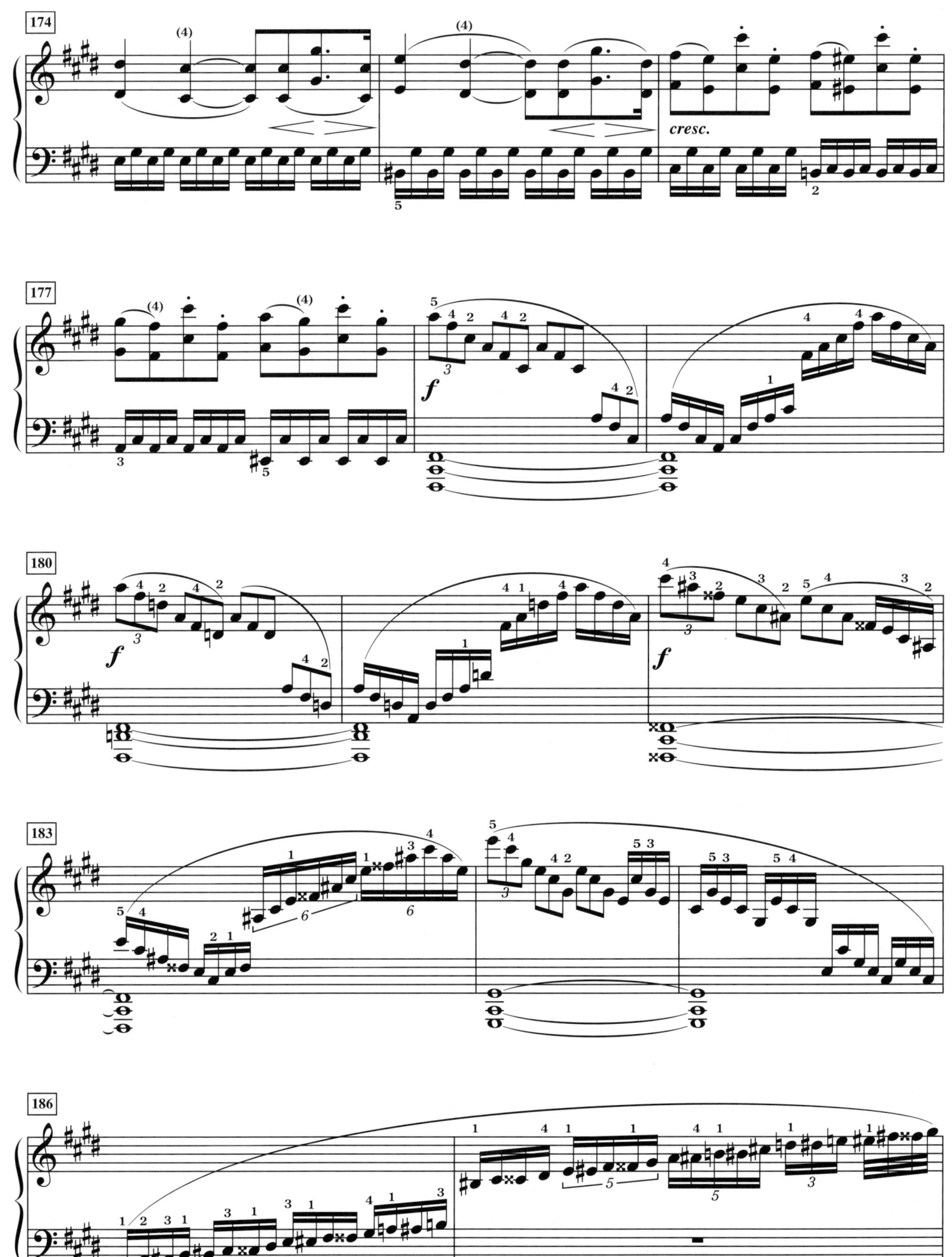

① The eleven referenced editors who suggest fingering for this trill all start on the main note. The cadenza that follows is marked *p* in the autograph, a mark that is omitted in the first edition. Only Schenker retains this mark. Casella mentions it in a footnote, but claims the composer "relinquished" it, offering no evidence. As for the cadenza itself, Tovey cautions against rhythmical division. Schnabel recommends triplets for its 27 eighth notes. Bülow writes out a sophisticated division:

About Op. 28

About Op. 28

The Op. 28 was written in the same period of time as the Op. 26 and the Op. 27 set. Although it is cast in a more traditional structure than its companions, the composer returning to the Classical four-movement idea of the first four sonatas, it nevertheless is regarded by many writers as belonging to the experimental group. This is mainly because the movements seem to be closely related in expressive intent, a reflective mood permeating the entire work.

The Op. 28 was published by the Bureau d'Arts et d'Industrie, the work having been announced in the *Wiener Zeitung* of Agusut 14, 1802 (along with the composer's transcription of the Op. 14, No. 1 for string quartet). The Bureau d'Arts et d'Industrie (or in German, Kunst- und Industrie-Comptoir) was founded in early 1802 and was administered by Joseph Schreyvogel, alias Thomas West (1768–1832), a well-known Viennese writer, and Jakob Hohler (n.d.), a dealer in fine arts, maps, and music. The firm published several of Beethoven's works between 1802 and 1808. Its future became uncertain following nationwide financial crises in 1811. In 1823, the firm and its publishing rights were taken over by S. A. Steiner & Co. Facsimiles of the autograph, the sketches, and the first edition of the Op. 28 were published by the Beethoven-Haus in 1996.[39]

The designation "Sonate pastorale" was first attached to the work by a London publisher, Broderip & Wilkinson, probably about 1805. It is thus quite possible that the composer was aware of this nickname. The name was reinforced in an 1838 edition published in Hamburg by August Cranz (1789–1870) with metronome markings by Beethoven's friend, the composer and pianist Ignaz Moscheles (1794–1870).

Op. 28 title page from the first edition, reproduced by kind permission from the copy in the Austrian National Library, Hoboken Collection, S. H. Beethoven 137

The Op. 28 is dedicated to Joseph Edlen von Sonnenfels (1732–1817), an important figure in governmental affairs. He held several high offices in the Austrian administration, was said to be a trusted advisor of Emperor Joseph II, became known as an advocate of penal reform, and was active in many philanthropic enterprises. Thus, he identified himself as a public figure who embraced the ideals of the enlightenment and a love for the arts. Although Beethoven usually dedicated his works as a result of patronage or as a way of expressing gratitude or friendship, he occasionally dedicated works to individuals who were not close to him personally, but whose idealism he admired. Apparently, such is the case in the dedication of the Op. 28, for whether or not the composer ever met Sonnenfels remains speculative.

---

[39] Beethoven, Ludwig van, *Piano Sonata, Op. 28.* Facsimile of the autograph, the sketches, and the first edition with transcription and commentary by Martha Frohlich (Bonn: Beethoven-Haus, 1996).

Sonata No. 15 in D Major (Grande Sonate), Op. 28

Autograph/facsimile:	survived
Sketches/loose pages:	movements 1, 2, 3, and 4
First edition:	Bureau d'Arts et d'Industrie: Vienna, 1802

The first movement, marked *Allegro*, is cast in a very traditional sonata-allegro form. Noteworthy is the fact that the first theme starts on a secondary dominant, moves through the subdominant and finally arrives at the home key of D major, all in the framework of the opening phrase of the work. Starting a work with some harmony from other than that of the tonic is unusual for the time. Beethoven's penchant for doing so occasionally shows itself in this work, as well as Op. 31, Nos. 2 and 3, Op. 101, and Op. 111. The first theme ends at measure 62, and the second theme area (measures 63–135) is also ushered in with a secondary dominant, this time of the subdominant in the key of A. The exposition ends with a short closing section (upbeat to measure 136–164). The development section (measures 165–269) makes use of the opening theme, particularly a fragment derived from its last measure. The recapitulation (measures 270–438) is regular. A coda based on the opening theme closes the movement (measures 439–462).

Beethoven's student Carl Czerny reports that Beethoven was very fond of playing the second movement (*Andante*) of this sonata.[40] It is cast in an **A B A** form, where each of these sections is a two-part structure, each part marked to be repeated. The movement is in D minor, and the **B** section (measures 25–42) is in the parallel major. In the return of **A** (at measure 43) the repeats are written out so that the composer may add figural variation. The coda (measures 87–103) makes use of thematic material from both the **A** and **B** sections.

The *Allegro vivace* scherzo movement is regular in structure. The repeat of the first section is written out so that the composer may add double notes throughout (measures 17–32). Similarly the second part of the trio section has its repeat written out so that the composer can vary the left-hand accompaniment, as well as the underlying harmonic progression (measures 87–94).

The final movement of this sonata, marked *Allegro ma non troppo*, is labeled *rondo* by the composer, and its structure is **A B A C A B A** coda. The opening theme makes use of a drone-like bass pattern, folk-like in character and perhaps the genesis of the sonata's nickname. The first **B** section (upbeat to measure 29–50) is in the dominant key. The **C** section (upbeats to measure 68–113) begins with a theme born of the rhythm of the bass pattern of the opening theme, but soon focuses on a more sustained idea presented with contrapuntal voice levels (starting at measure 79). The final return of **A** (upbeat to measure 169–192) is varied and is in the key of G major rather than the tonic (D major). It leads to the dominant of the home key, however, creating suspense for the coda, marked at a faster tempo, and serving to bring the work to a brilliant close (measures 193–210).

---

[40] Czerny, Op. cit., p.51

Dedicated to Joseph Edlen von Sonnenfels

Sonata No. 15 in D Major
(Grande Sonate)

Ludwig van Beethoven (1770–1827)
Op. 28

ⓐ Measures 178–223 are missing from the autograph, but appear in the first edition. Scholarly speculation has suggested the section is missing because a page got lost in the process of revising the passage, or as a result of the fact that the composer changed to a different stock of manuscript paper at precisely this point. Virtually all editions follow the first edition and include these measures.

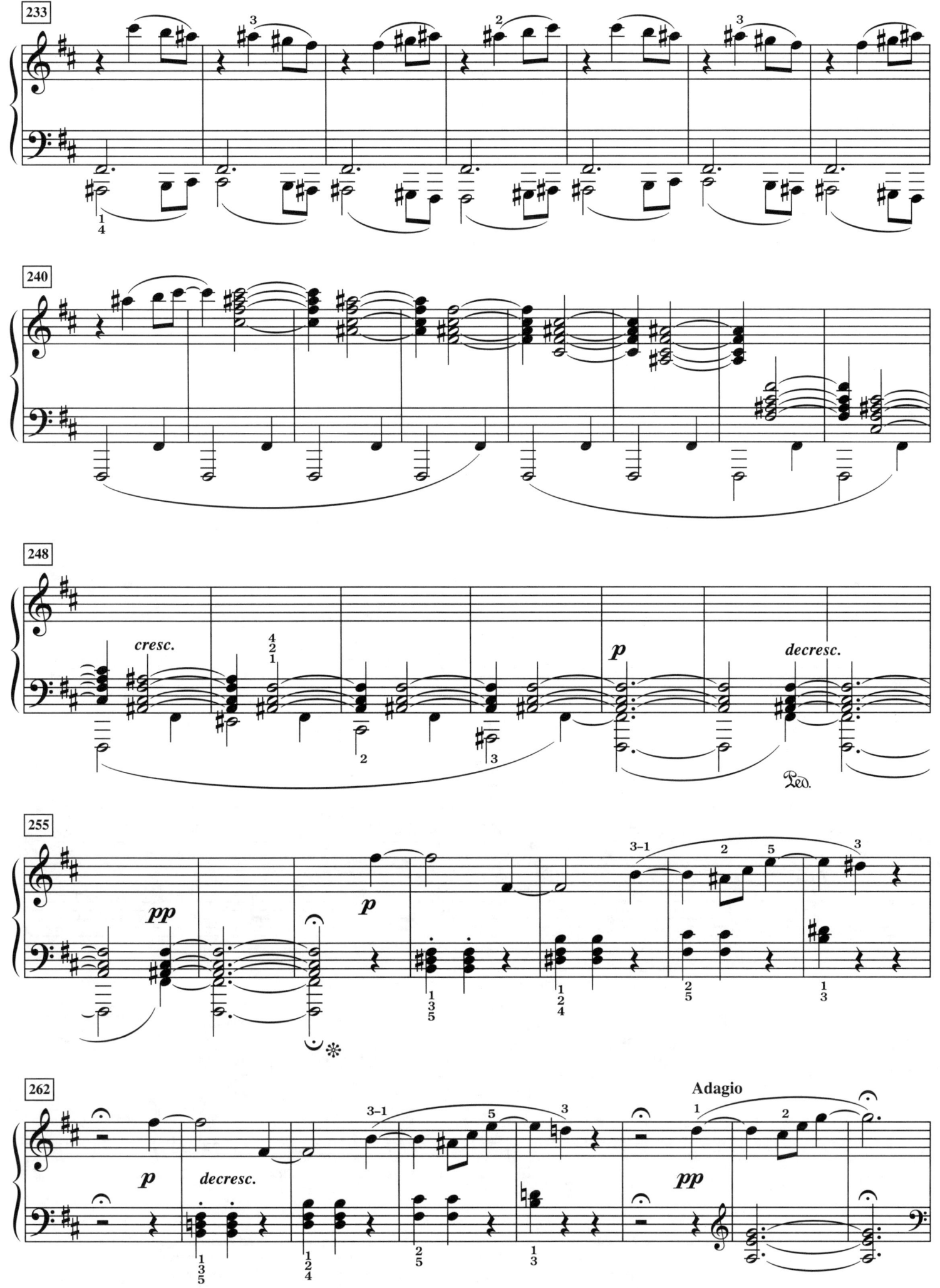

ⓑ This phrase in the exposition extends to the end of the measure, stopping at the last eighth note (see measure 27). Here it ends at the first eighth note of the measure. Several such inconsistencies in phrasing and articulation exist between the exposition and the recapitulation. Since there is no way of determining why these exist or if one or another version is in error, the markings have been left as they appear in the autograph and the first edition.

ⓒ The autograph and the first edition show *f* in measure 333. Bülow, Casella, Schenker, and Schnabel change the marking to *sf* to make it consistent with the marking in measure 58.

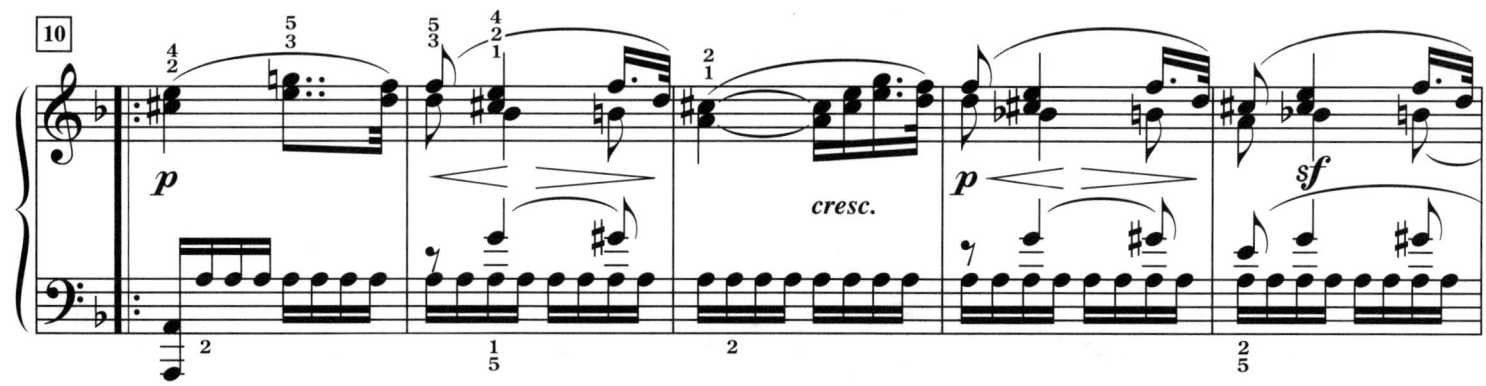
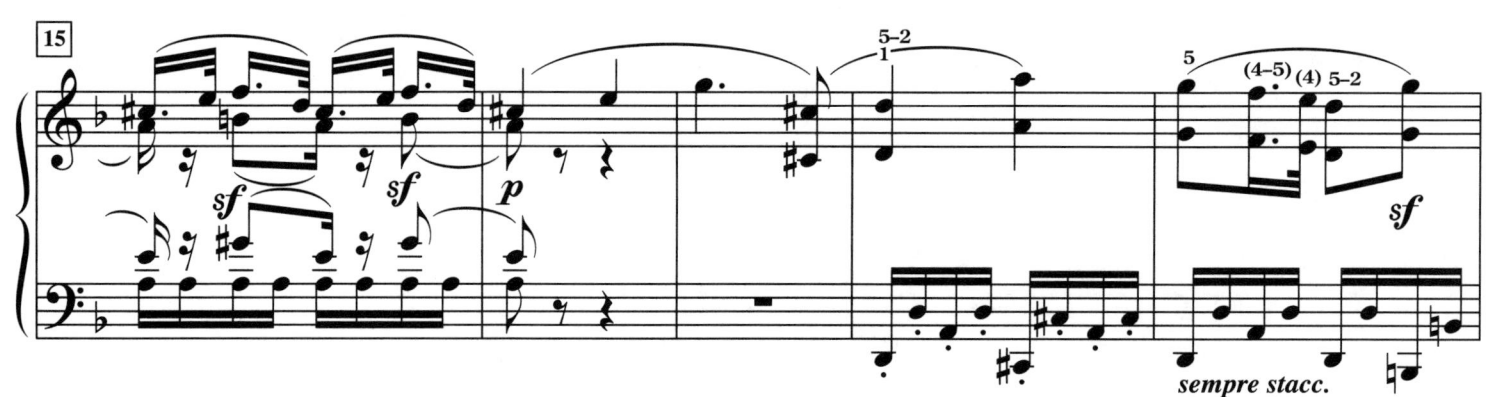

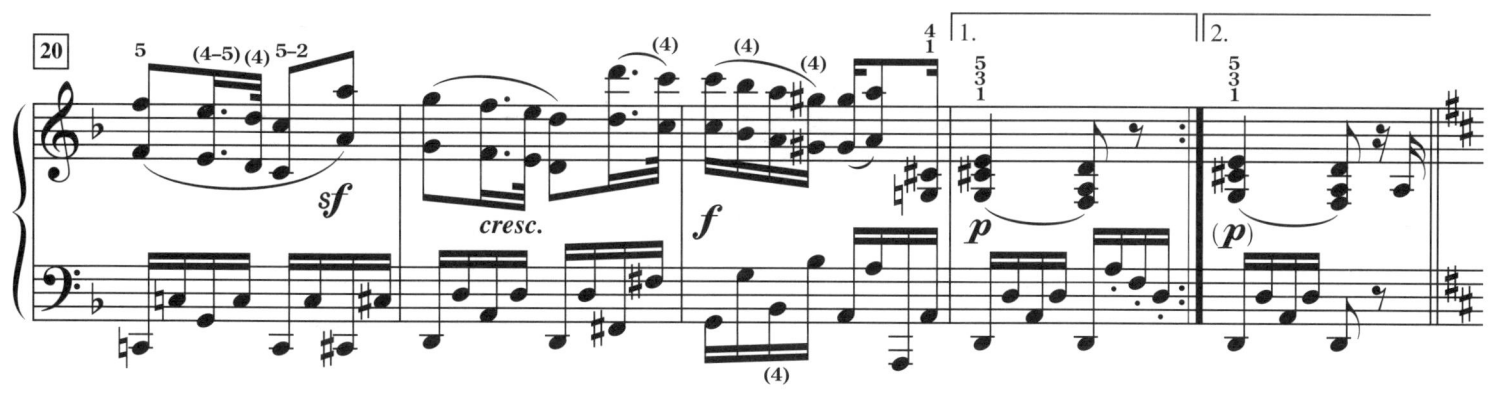
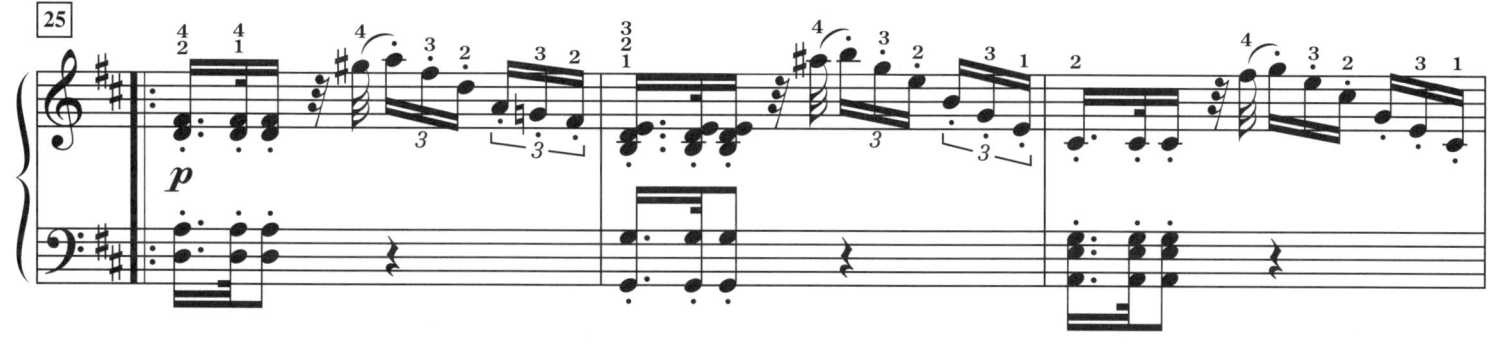

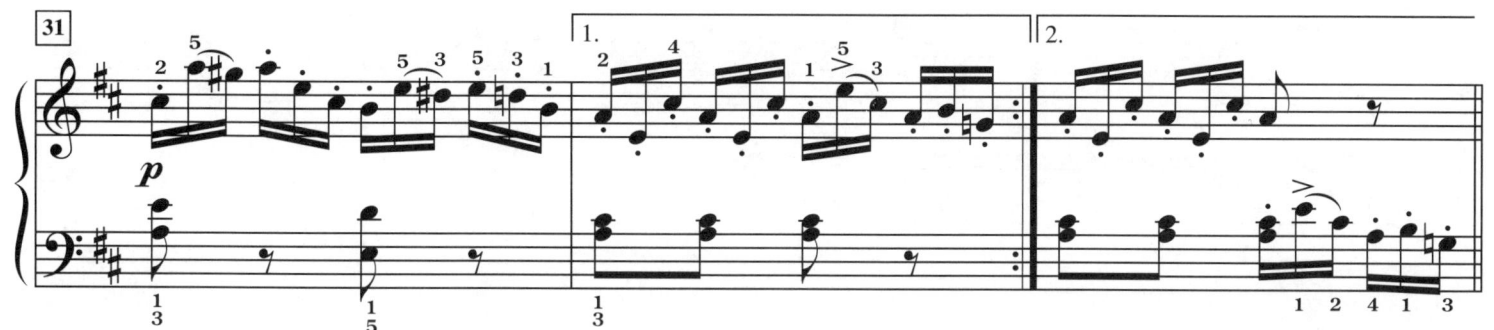

ⓐ Beethoven's marks in the autograph on the second sixteenth note of beat 2 in measures 28, 32, and 33 are slightly larger than normal accents. This led the engraver of the first edition to interpret them as decrescendo marks. Of the referenced editors, nine and this editor believe the marks to be accents. Arrau, Martienssen, and Schenker follow the first edition, indicating decrescendo markings.

autograph measure 28:

first edition measure 28:

(b) A natural sign followed by a sharp sign appears in both the first edition and the autograph. Of the editors who deal with this turn in detail, d'Albert, Casella, Geoffroy, Köhler, Schenker, and Tovey indicate using a B-natural in the turn, Casella even making a case for it in a footnote. Bülow and Schnabel use the B-sharp. This editor sides with the first group, believing the ambiguity is to be read as a B-natural followed by a C-sharp. Rhythmic realizations differ, from the most rapid of Bülow, who confines the turn to the second sixteenth of beat 2, to the broadest of d'Albert, who simply uses four thirty-second notes starting on beat 2. Schnabel's rhythmic arrangement lends a feeling of improvisation and is attractive to this editor:

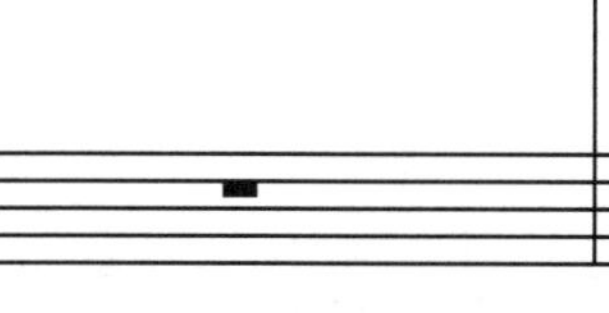

A second confusing issue is a cresc. placed over the last two notes of the measure in the first edition. This indication would seem to be in conflict with the decrescendo mark placed between the staves in the same portion of the measure. The autograph does not show the cresc. at this point, so one can assume its addition was an engraver's error. The error is, however, incorporated into Arrau's edition. Wallner includes it in her 1952 edition, but deletes it in the 1980 version.

ⓐ The first edition shows a cresc. in measure 31, and many editions include this mark. It does not appear in the autograph.

(a) There is confusion regarding the slurring at the end of measure 30 and the beginning of measure 31. The autograph shows the two slurs attending the voices in the treble clef ending on the last eighth note of measure 30. A new slur in the bass clef begins on the same beat. New slurs begin in the treble clef on the downbeat of measure 31. Examination of analogous measures 146–147 does not help, for the composer, in what appears to be hasty notation, writes one long slur for the upper voice from beat 6 of measure 144 through beat 6 of measure 146. The slur for the middle voice begins on beat 6 of measure 145 and ends on beat 4 of measure 146. The slurring in the first edition is also erratic, showing the upper-voice slur in measure 30 ending on the quarter note of beat 4 and the middle-voice slur ending on the eighth note of beat 6. There is no slur at all in the bass clef part in measure 30, the slur starting simultaneously with the middle voice on the downbeat of measure 31. In the analogous measures (146–147) of the first edition, the pattern used in the autograph for measures 30–31 is followed. Moreover, the tie in the upper voice between the eighth note on beat 6 of measure 30 and the dotted quarter note of measure 31 is missing in measures 146–147 in both the autograph and the first edition. Various editors have reconciled these irregularities in different ways. The representation in this edition is one that is also used by d'Albert, Arrau, Bülow, Geoffroy, and Wallner (1980).

(b) Of the referenced editors, eight indicate fingering for this trill that suggests starting on the main note. Only Arrau's fingering suggests starting on the upper note. This editor suggests the following realization, which may also be applied in measure 159:

(c) The slurring in the RH of measure 54 differs from that of all other statements of this phrase (measures 3, 7, 58, 116, and 120). The change is shown in both the autograph and the first edition. Of the referenced editors, d'Albert, Geoffroy, Krebs, and Wallner incorporate it without comment. The others alter the measure to conform to its counterparts. This editor has remained true to the sources. The performer will have to decide whether or not the change should influence how the measure is to be played.

ⓓ Two autograph versions of this episode exist. One of them ties the two B's in the upper voice between measures 81 and 82. The other does not, nor is there a tie in the first edition.

ⓔ The autograph at this point has something scratched out and *più allegro quasi presto* written in the margin. The first edition incorporates the indication. Notwithstanding this evidence, Bülow and Tovey show only *più allegro* and the latter argues for its authenticity in a note. The dynamic mark *p* appears in the first edition. It is doubtful that this mark is in the autograph, the heavy *p* there looking like the first letter of the word *più* in the new tempo designation. Nevertheless, all of the referenced editors incorporate the dynamic marking from the first edition, and this editor concurs that starting the passage *piano* is a good idea, given the ensuing direction to crescendo.

autograph measure 192:

first edition measure 193: